MW01133747

Fenton
Basket Patterns
Acanthus to Hummingbird

Debbie and Randy Coe

4880 Lower Valley Road, Atglen, PA 19310 USA

Dedication

We dedicate this book to all the talented employees who are responsible for Fenton's success in the marketplace. In particular, we honor Howard Seufer and Pam Dick, who gave considerable help to us in obtaining information. Howard Seufer is a retired employee who spent countless hours obtaining photographs for us at the factory. His attention to detail enabled us to have photographs of glass production that we would not otherwise have had. Pam Dick is Frank M. Fenton's assistant with a very demanding job, yet she spent many hours locating information for us. They each spent several days getting the special order baskets organized and photographed from the museum. We cherish them both and appreciate their devotion to this book.

Library of Congress Cataloging-in-Publication Data

Coe, Debbie.
  Fenton basket patterns : acanthus to hummingbird / by Debbie and Randy Coe.
     p. cm.
  ISBN 0-7643-2272-9 (hardcover)
1. Fenton Art Glass Company—Catalogs. 2. Baskets, Glass—West Virginia—Williamstown—Catalogs. 3. Baskets, Glass—Collectors and collecting—United States—Catalogs. I. Coe, Randy. II. Title.

NK5198.F4C64 2005
748.2'09754'22—dc22
                                        2005003046

Designed by Mark David Bowyer
Type set in Americana XBd BT / Zurich BT

ISBN: 0-7643-2272-9
Printed in China
1 2 3 4

Published by Schiffer Publishing Ltd.
4880 Lower Valley Road
Atglen, PA 19310
Phone: (610) 593-1777; Fax: (610) 593-2002
E-mail: Info@schifferbooks.com

For the largest selection of fine reference books on this and related subjects, please visit our web site at
www.schifferbooks.com
We are always looking for people to write books on new and related subjects. If you have an idea for a book please contact us at the above address.

This book may be purchased from the publisher.
Include $3.95 for shipping.
Please try your bookstore first.
You may write for a free catalog.

In Europe, Schiffer books are distributed by
Bushwood Books
6 Marksbury Ave.
Kew Gardens
Surrey TW9 4JF England
Phone: 44 (0) 20 8392-8585; Fax: 44 (0) 20 8392-9876
E-mail: info@bushwoodbooks.co.uk
Free postage in the U.K., Europe; air mail at cost.

Contents

Preface

Frank Leslie Fenton graduated from high school in 1897 and was the class valedictorian. He briefly thought about being a teacher before following the desire to be in the glass business. He did an apprenticeship at Indiana Glass and two years later became the foreman there. As the new company of Jefferson Glass opened its doors in 1900, Frank L. felt a need for change and was there ready to work. In 1903, Frank moved on to Bastow Glass in Coudersport, Pennsylvania. After Bastow was destroyed fire in 1904, Frank L. Fenton went over to Northwood Glass in Wheeling, West Virginia to find employment. While utilizing his skills there, Frank L. Fenton soon realized that he could make better use of his own ability and work for himself. Frank L. and his brother John Fenton made a decision that would forever alter the local economy. Together they pooled their money and opened an account on May 4, 1905 at the Dollar Bank in Wheeling with only $284.86. The Fenton Art Glass Company was now established. Fenton has been lucky. Through many trials, tribulations and successes, Fenton is still here, family owned and providing employment to the West Virginia economy. They are succeeding when others have not. With this publication, we celebrate their Centennial.

Acknowledgments

Both sets of our children, Myra and Stephen Hixson along with Tara and Jeff McRitchie, have their own collections of glass that they share with you here. Their generosity is really appreciated. We are so grateful for them to live so close that we are able to see them on a regular basis. All of our lives get so busy but we need to stay in connection with the ones we love. They are the love of our life and we feel truly blessed.

All of the following people either brought baskets to our house to photograph, allowed us to come to their home to photograph or allowed us to photograph them at a show or at the Pacific Northwest Fenton Association (PNWFA) annual convention. With these people's generosity, this book contains a vast assortment of beautiful baskets. A giant thank you to: Agnes Allison; Darlene & Gordon Cochran; Virginia Domingo; John Fallihee; Mary Walrath Jachim; Debbie & Ed Lane; Leota McLean; Donna & Ron Miller; Barbara & Ed Nunes; Emily Osterman; Jackie Shirley; Jack & Jackie Skaw; and Juanita Williams.

John Gager was such a great asset to our Fenton research project. His tireless effort to develop and maintain the Fenton Fanatics website is simply amazing. This site has so much information to offer. For us, to obtain the complete list of QVC baskets was a snap. At the site you go to the QVC database. To search, you list the things you are looking for. In our search, we entered "basket" in the mould slot and then the year. Out came a list of all the baskets for that particular year, including the mould shape, number, color, date, price, and signature, if any. Then, you can highlight the basket to see what it looks like. We so appreciate John's countless hours spent keeping this site up to date. John also let us photograph any baskets he had.

Marian Thorton owns two huge Fenton shops: Collectors Showcase in Centralia and Snohomish, both in Washington state. She turned the Centralia shop over to us for photography. We had so many beautiful baskets to photograph in one place that we felt we were in glass heaven.

John Walk is another person we could count on at any time. He generously supplied us with some baskets to photograph that we were not able to find in our area. This sharing of information between authors helps all of our jobs go so much easier.

All of the Fenton family members were such a valuable resource to us. Frank Fenton went above and beyond the call of duty spending countless hours finding information about the workers and basket origins. Questions went out to him and answers came back; many times an answer generated another question. We are sure Frank thought he was back in school with an endless pile of homework assignments. He thought we were crazy to categorize Fenton baskets, since so many don't fit any category or they fall into several. We appreciate Frank proofreading all of our material. His love of his company and the glass they have made was evident in all of his answers.

Nancy and George Fenton were terrific in furnishing information about themselves and about the company. Deciding what type of basket to offer in what color is a daunting task. George and Nancy have spent many hours studying marketing trends to see that their products have appeal to the current decorating theme. Their insight was greatly appreciated and we thank them for proofreading our material and providing the Foreword.

In addition, the following Fenton family members took time from their busy schedules to furnish us with information about themselves, the family, the company positions, and other interesting facts. Their assistance to our project is greatly appreciated. A huge thank you goes to Christine Fenton, Lynn Fenton Erb, Mike Fenton, Randy Fenton, Scott Fenton, Shelley Fenton Ash, and Tom Fenton.

Suzi Whitaker and Jon Saffell, from the design department, each furnished us with information about themselves and their various projects.

All the ladies from the decorating department, Kim Barley, Frances Burton, C. C. Hardman, Robin Spindler and Stacy Williams, furnished information about themselves and their favorite baskets. Jennifer Maston provided information about the museum and the guests who have viewed glass there.

Bob and Pat Hill provided us with information about themselves and their jobs at Fenton. Their daughter, Amber, was very helpful in keeping track of new baskets in the Fenton Gift Shop that we needed to photograph.

Pam Dick was of enormous help spending countless hours rounding up over 300 baskets from the museum and obtaining the background information on each one. Howard Seufer, now retired from Fenton, came to our assistance by photographing many scenes around the factory, various family members, and the baskets from the museum. He worked many long hours with Pam to get the shots right. It was especially nice to have these super people, with great devotion, helping us.

Foreword

Baskets are a hallmark of the Fenton Art Glass Company. From the first handled basket made by Frank Meyers in 1939 through our production today, the Fenton company has taken great pride in developing ever-changing styles of baskets and handles.

Handling baskets is a highly skilled craft and one most enjoyed by visitors to the Fenton factory. They, and we, are continually amazed at the deft workmanship needed to turn a fiery liquid ribbon into a perfectly arched handle in a few short seconds.

The thickness and height of each handle is evaluated to create the correct balance and proportion for the finished basket. Two or more handle designs may be sampled on a piece before we achieve the correct proportion. Occasionally, we even use a crystal handle on a dark color to maintain the correct balance for the basket.

Handlers are justifiably proud of their work. When a handler designs his own personal stamp, it becomes his signature of craftsmanship to the world. This book showcases the evolution of Fenton basket design and craftsmanship through the past sixty-plus years.

We appreciate the work that Debbie and Randy Coe have put into compiling this book and hope that readers gain a new appreciation for the variety and skill of the Fenton handlers and the glassmaking teams they work with.

George and Nancy Fenton
November, 2004

Introduction

This project began as an effort to document American-made glass baskets. As we progressed, something unexpected happened. When we started counting baskets to see how many we had for each company, Fenton greatly outnumbered all the rest we had photographed. All of a sudden, we had to reexamine what we wanted to do. With Fenton's 100th anniversary approaching, we decided to focus on Fenton for this book. They are still in business when many of the other companies are not. When you look at all of the glass houses that have come on gone, you find so many that never reached the amazing 100-year mark. We wanted to also explore the background and history of Fenton baskets. It was interesting to learn about so many of the patterns. Other facts we have to share include how handler marks were developed, when and how logos came into existence, why there are so many beautiful colors, and facts not found in other books. Many Fenton employees should be acknowledged for their roles in the production of baskets. Peviously unknown workers are now recognized and honored for their contributions to the success of this company.

After compiling the information and photographs, it became obvious that there was too much for a single book. The last thing we wanted was to harm the integrity of our original vision. If we eliminated any patterns or background material, we thought we would be discrediting the Fenton Art Glass Company and the many baskets they have produced. So it was decided to have two volumes of the work. This first volume features the patterns from Acanthus to Hummingbird. The second volume features the patterns from Innovation to Wisteria and the numbered patterns. We are pleased to present these beautiful baskets for your enjoyment.

Measurements

Actual height and width measurements were taken of each piece of glass as it was photographed. Like all handmade glass, slight variations will exist in size from one piece to the next. If the handle is taller, the width might be smaller. If the handle is shorter, the width might be wider. When the shape is irregular, the larger measurement was used.

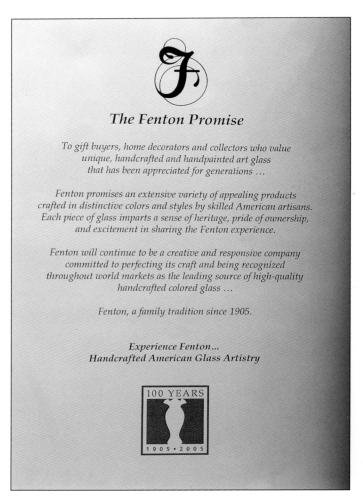

The Fenton Promise

To gift buyers, home decorators and collectors who value unique, handcrafted and handpainted art glass that has been appreciated for generations ...

Fenton promises an extensive variety of appealing products crafted in distinctive colors and styles by skilled American artisans. Each piece of glass imparts a sense of heritage, pride of ownership, and excitement in sharing the Fenton experience.

Fenton will continue to be a creative and responsive company committed to perfecting its craft and being recognized throughout world markets as the leading source of high-quality handcrafted colored glass ...

Fenton, a family tradition since 1905.

Experience Fenton...
Handcrafted American Glass Artistry

100 YEARS
1905•2005

A reprint of the Fenton Promise Reprinted with permission from the Fenton Art Glass Company.

Value Guide

The values given in this book are for glassware in *mint condition* only. Any type of damage, such as a chip or crack, greatly diminishes the value of the piece. For practical purposes, any damage leaves the basket with only minimal value, if any at all. Pieces that have been repaired should reflect a far-below-normal value, depending on their appearance.

The front view of the Fenton factory

We have asked both collectors and dealers to contribute values so we could obtain a true reflection of the current market. The listed values have been derived from actual dealer sales, what collectors have paid, prices seen at shows, auction results, and national publications. Some of the pieces were not found in secondary market prices, so the value listed here was based upon the original selling price. As with any type of collectible glass, there are some regional differences in supply and demand.

A collector ultimately needs to decide what he would be willing pay for a specific item. The authors have tried to list sustainable values, not ones for an isolated basket selling for a record amount. Their job was to report the prices that were found, not to set values based on their opinions. This book is to be used only as guide when determining what an item is worth, based on available information. Many older baskets have appreciated in value because of the cost of a similar new basket. Prices do go up and down depending on the supply and demand for the piece. This fact is not popular, but one that has became a reality for most dealers and collectors.

Neither the authors nor the publishers assume any responsibility for transactions that may occur because of this book.

Logos

In the initial years, Fenton only marked their glass by paper labels. It was only after Fenton decided to reissue carnival glass in 1970 was the decision made to actually put a mark in the glass. At first only the new carnival glass pieces were marked to distinguish the new ones from the old. This idea proved to be very popular among collectors. Starting in 1974, Fenton started marking all of their glass. The following is a list of logos and how they are used.

Fenton logo for the 1970s

Fenton logo for the 1980s

The 75th designation was put on items celebrating the 75th anniversary in 1980

The 80th designation was added to items for the 80th anniversary collection of 1985

Fenton logo for the 1990s

Fenton logo for the 1990s that is sandblasted on pieces that don't allow the logo to be seen otherwise.

The 90th designation was added to items in 1995 Historic Collection celebrating the 90th anniversary.

The 95th designation was added to items in the 2000 Historic Collections celebrating the 95th anniversary.

The script F was sand blasted on blown items that didn't allow the regular logo to be seen.

This mark was used on any mould that had been purchased since 1983 and was not a Fenton original.

The capital "F" was used on items in the gift shop to indicate a preferred second since 1998.

The stars whether solid or open were used to indicate a preferred second quality item in the gift shop from 1996 to 1998.

This logo is currently being used to indicate items from 2000 to 2009.

Chapter 1
Fenton Personnel

Family Members

Left to Right: Nancy Fenton; Frank Fenton; George Fenton

Frank M. Fenton signature

George Fenton signature

Frank M. Fenton

Frank and his brother Bill grew up among six sisters. Eight kids created many interesting moments. Frank gained a lot experience spending summers working at the factory. Initially in the 1930s, Frank spent time actually in the factory. Later, he moved back to the office learning how to figure the payroll and attended his first wage conference in 1937 with his father. He became assistant general manager in 1942. At the time of his father's death in 1948, Frank was only thirty two and elected to be the company president, treasurer and general manager. About six months later, Robert C. Fenton Sr. passed away and Bill then became vice president and secretary. Frank was responsible for the purchase of moulds from Rubel, Paden City, Verlys, and U.S. Glass. Charlie Goe was hired by Frank to develop new glass formulas. The decorating department with Louise Piper had been reset up because of Frank. When his wife Elizabeth fell ill in 1978, Frank resigned as president so he could spend more time with her. Later after her death in 1980, he continued as Chairman of the board. One of his goals was to create a Fenton museum. He later became the company historian. Frank has been a speaker at many events. Frank is so willing to answer any question on glass whether it be Fenton or glass from another company. Frank always wants to make sure the answers to questions are correct. He is the most generous man with the sharing of information. Frank is at the factory every day to assist with whatever comes up and to go through his large stack of mail. Frank also works with the Special Orders Department to assist collector organizations in having their special pieces made. Frank's vast years of experience and knowledge are such a great asset to any collector.

One of Frank's favorite baskets is the Paneled #C65746P, that was done in 1993 for QVC. It is in the Persian Pearl color, with a Plum crest and colored with grapes.

George Fenton

George was one of four boys born to Frank M. and Elizabeth Fenton. He grew up around the factory and did odd jobs at first. George attended Wesleyan College and graduated with honors in 1971. With a degree in physics and astronomy, he joined the company full time in 1972. For a while he was Frank's assistant, doing project work in several areas of the factory including blow shop production, union relations, and industrial engineering. He held line responsibilities as Decorating Foreman in 1976 and became Manager of Manufacturing in 1979. Being involved with several different types of jobs gave him a real feel for the workings of the factory. By 1985, George had moved into the position of Executive Vice President. When uncle Bill stepped down as president in 1986, George assumed the job of president of the company. George had the definite advantage over his father when he assumed the presidency. This time there were many family members to turn to when a question or a problem came up. In looking to spur growth for the rest of the 1980s and 1990s, George encouraged new colors and enhanced decorating techniques. In 1989, he completed the Owner/President Management Program at Harvard Business School. George feels the pride of Fenton employees shows through in their products and enables the company to promote their products more effectively. During the year, George remains visible to collectors by appearing at signing events and speaking at conventions.

George and his wife Nancy have two sons, Ben and David, and a granddaughter, Audrey. He enjoys golf and basketball along with family skiing trips. His favorite Fenton colors are Favrene, Topaz Amberina and old carnival. There are a couple of baskets that he especially likes: the #6831U5 Burmese with the Bluebird design from the 1999 Connoisseur line and the #CV300T7 Cobalt overlay with the threaded handle that was done for QVC.

Nancy Fenton signature

Nancy Fenton

Nancy first became acquainted with George Fenton at age thirteen when her family moved next door to George's family. They immediately began dating and were married after Nancy graduated from Denison University in 1972. Nancy continued gaining experience by doing marketing work through Ohio University. She started doing research into buying patterns in the consumer market. This experience led her to be hired in the Fenton sales department in 1982. In 1985, she became new product development manager. Her most exciting projects have been the continuing development of new colors as well as encouraging the redevelopment of older Fenton favorites. The highlight of a color project was working with Bud Ward, hot metal supervisor, to refine Favrene so it could be offered in the line. As Director of Design, Nancy is constantly searching for new ideas and trends in the market place that can be used at Fenton. Nancy enjoys seeing what the current colors are and how they can be adapted to Fenton glass. She is also involved with Fenton family signing events across the country and likes to talk to collectors about what they would like to see made in Fenton glass.

Nancy and her husband, George, have two sons, Ben and David, and one granddaughter, Audrey. Her favorite outdoor things are ski trips and a round of golf. Favorite Fenton colors are Favrene, Mandarin Red

and Ruby Amberina Stretch. Some of her favorite baskets are: #5739NH Rosemilk Drapery with the green crest and any of the #9544 Vulcan ones from the late 1980s and early 1990s.

Tom Fenton signature

Tom Fenton

Tom is the son of Frank M. and Elizabeth Fenton. He graduated from Ohio Wesleyan University and then went on to the Ohio University Grad School. He joined the US Army Reserves. For several years he was a representative on the board of the Glass Manufacturing Industry Council (GMIC). This organization encompasses all major aspects of the American glass

Back - Left to Right: Randy Fenton; Tom Fenton; Mike Fenton; Scott Fenton
Front - Left to Right: Shelley Fenton Ash; Christine Fenton; Lynn Fenton Erb

industry by encouraging cooperation in the environment, productivity and technology.

He is Vice President of Manufacturing. He works with the hot metal superintendent. Recently he oversaw the factory expansion, repairs and continuous furnace reconstruction. "Our goal is to constantly improve the product we make for Fenton's followers throughout the world. Crucial to the achievement of high quality, at a reasonable cost, is the Fenton craftsman's skill for quickly executing new designs," Tom has stated.

Tom and his wife, Sharon have three adult children and three precious grandchildren. They both enjoy hiking and traveling. For many years Tom has worked with artisan Dave Fetty. He really likes some of the off hand items.

Mike Fenton signature

Mike Fenton

Mike is the son of Frank M. and Elizabeth Fenton. At age nineteen in 1964, he became a shipping department stock boy at Fenton. He attended the College of Wooster and Marietta College. Mike served in the Navy from 1967 to 1971 with two Pacific tours. Upon being discharged, he returned to the company to work as the Purchasing Manager. He next moved on to be Fenton's Safety Director in 1985. As recognition for his work in 1996, Mike was a nominee for West Virginia's *"Safety Professional of the Year"* award. Mike is currently the Safety Director and Purchasing Manager. Keeping the work environment safe and ensuring that the company doesn't run short of purchased supplies constantly vie for Mike's time.

Mike and his wife, Kathy, have two daughters, Meredith and Natalie. Mike has a third daughter, Kerry, from a previous marriage. Meredith's three year old son, Isaiah, is Mike's first grandson. Daughter Natalie, a professional ballerina, was Jon Saffell's model for the ballerina figurine, appropriately called Natalie. She just presented Mike with a new grandson, Mason, in July 2004. Fenton's first chemist

Jacob Rosenthal, built a house in 1908. Mike and his family had the proud privilege of living in this Williamstown house from 1977 to 2003.

Mike's favorite hobbies include photography, basketball, and camping with his family. With a grandson in Washington, D.C. and another in northwest Montana, traveling now seems to be added to his list of hobbies. Mike also enjoys designing lamps for the company. He designed five of the seven metal assemblies pictured in the 2004 catalog.

Pitcher sets are among Mike's favorite types of glass. His favorite treatment is stretch glass. One of Mike's most memorable work experiences involved the #3734 milk glass 12" hobnail basket. In 1971 he was the "Working Foreman" responsible for loading 25,000 baskets into nine railroad boxcars. These were to fill an order for "S & H" green stamps. Each basket was individually boxed in the packing department, moved to the upstairs of the shipping department and then rolled down a 100 foot outside conveyor to the rail siding next to Hot Metal. The boxes were then stacked in the boxcars until each car was totally filled to the ceiling. Wow, that was a lot of glass in one spot.

Randy Fenton signature

Randy Fenton

Randy is the son of the late Bill Fenton. He worked in the gift shop while in high school and college. In 1975, he graduated from Marietta College with a degree in business management. He started to work with his brother Don in sales. Nine years later he went back to the gift shop. Randy is currently the Fenton Gift Shop Vice-President/Treasurer. Most people don't realize it but the Fenton Gift Shop and the Fenton Art Glass Company are actually two separate corporations. The Fenton Gift Shop buys glass from the company just like any other customer.

Like his late father Bill, Randy likes Burmese glass but Chocolate glass is his number one choice. Other favorites include Cranberry Opalescent and Rosalene.

Randy and his wife Debbie have three children; Cassy, Danielle, and Justin. Some of Randy's favorite decorations involve the beauty of the out of doors.

Shelley Fenton Ash

Christine Fenton signature

Shelley Fenton Ash

Shelley is the youngest daughter of the late Bill Fenton. While a youngster, Shelley appeared in several different catalogs. In 1961 at the age of 3 1/2, Shelley appeared in the first Fenton catalog advertising Milk Glass Hobnail. On the 1962 catalog, she appeared on the cover. In 1963, she was shown with courting lamps and a Hobnail vanity set. Shelley can be seen holding a Silver Crest basket in the 1964 catalog. At age sixteen, Shelley again appeared in another catalog, this time advertising picture frames.

While in high school and college, the summers were spent being a tour guide. She graduated in 1980 from West Virginia University with a degree in Marketing. After graduation she joined the sales department. She attended gift shows, worked with sales representatives and helped with catalogs. Shelley became an assistant sales manager in 1985.

Shelley currently has multi task positions. She is the Graphics Manager and QVC Product Coordinator. For the graphics part, Shelley enjoys working with the photographer and designing the company catalogs, supplements and brochures. In addition, she is responsible for developing the new items for QVC shows as well as for QVC.com. Shelley also serves on a design committee that oversees the new moulds and also the new items that go into the regular line.

Shelley is married and with her husband, Danny, have an indoor air quality company. They also have three children: Amanda, Alex, and Ellie, who keep them plenty busy when not at work. Daughter Ellie has followed in her mother's footsteps by appearing in a Fenton catalog. Ellie is shown in the 2000 catalog holding a mini bear and mini cat as part of the Simple Pleasures displays.

Among her favorite baskets are those in her favorite colors of Ruby Amberina Stretch and Ruby Carnival, Gold and Royal Purple. The fall colors are among Shelley's favorites.

Shelley loves the large ribbon candy crimp baskets with colored crests. Her favorite is the large Topaz basket, done in 1998 as a limited edition for Easter that also had her signature on it.

Christine Fenton

Christine is the daughter of the late Bill Fenton. Like other family members, she spent summers from high school and college working at the company. After college graduation she went to work for Union Carbide and spent seven years there. In 1975, she started work in the Fenton Gift Shop. Christine switched over to customer service in 1980. Things became so busy that finally a toll free 800 number had to be set up. She was part of that transition time. Today, she is responsible for the Gift Shop Personnel/ Data Processing. She is also a Night Manager one night each week.

One of her favorite type of items is the tobacco jars, she began collecting in the 1970s. She puts them to use by storing treats in them for her furry kids: several cats and a dog. Her favorite color is the Rosalene. The Rosalene Chessie box is among her top choices of special pieces.

Though claiming not to be actually a basket collector, she does have a number of baskets in her home. Christine says, "I love our overlay baskets and ones with the ringed edge. I have some offhand baskets that have been made over the years. I also love our miniature baskets in many beautiful colors and patterns."

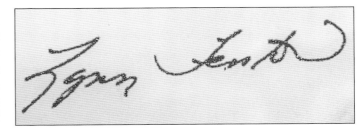

Lynn Fenton Erb signature

Lynn Fenton Erb

Lynn is the granddaughter of Frank M. Fenton. Her father Frank R. Fenton became interested in animal husbandry and pursued that as a profession. In 1994, Lynn became the first fourth family generation member to join the company.

She had received her Bachelor of Arts from Bowling Green State University and her Masters in International Management from Thunderbird. She had first worked for Electronic Data Systems for seven years. There she gained experience of manufacturing facilities.

Lynn started her work at Fenton as part of the sales and marketing team and developed the company's new collector newsletter, Glass Messenger. She next moved on to gain some experience in the manufacturing part of the company. Lynn worked in the program of Continuous Improvement of Quality and has overseen the Decorating Services Department.

Currently, she is Assistant to the President. Her duties involve giving support to the Engineering Department and devising for the Decorating Department new management support processes. She and her husband, Eric have two daughters, Elissa and Isabelle, fifth generation family members. Her favorite types of glass are stretch and perfume bottles. She really likes the different examples of whimsey baskets and the first Glass Messenger exclusive, a hand painted Cranberry basket.

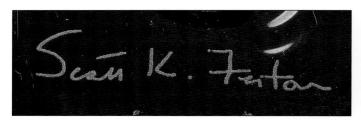

Scott Fenton signature

Scott K. Fenton

Scott is the son of Tom Fenton and is the second fourth family generation member to join the company. While growing up, Scott spent holidays and summers doing various jobs at the factory. After turning sixteen, he dusted shelves in the gift shop and gave factory tours. Later jobs were spent in inventory control, packing & shipping, and hot metal. Scott, then moved on to do some work for his father, Tom Fenton, Vice President of Manufacturing. These projects included researching glass temperatures for different types of glass and employee relations. He graduated in 1997 from West Virginia Wesleyan College. He is currently the National Sales Manager in charge of overseeing channels of distribution across the United States.

Scott and his wife, Grace, became very proud parents in 2002 of Jackson Kittrell Fenton, the newest fifth generation member. A full picture of Jackson is displayed by the Inspirations line in the 2004

catalog. Scott's home is decorated with mainly Hanging Heart pieces and trinket boxes. His wife, Grace, is a big trinket collector. His favorite shape in baskets is the new drapery pattern, produced recently in Cranberry. Scott said, "that could change though, since there are a few in the works though that will probably replace it as #1."

In Remembrance

When we started working on this project, both Bill and Don were active family members of the Fenton Art Glass Company. Bill was most visible as the spokesman for QVC. After an illness, Bill Fenton passed away in December, 2002. Don Fenton, Vice President of Sales, went in the hospital for bypass surgery. The surgery had gone well, but an aneurysm developed and Don died February 3, 2003. Both now are in God's hands and have eternal life. They are missed everyday.

Skilled Workers

Jon Saffell, Fenton Art Glass designer

Jon Saffell

In 1957, Jon started work in the design department at Fostoria Glass. He was promoted to Design Department Manager and then later to Director of Design. Jon was married to Carolyn in 1960. He and Carolyn have been blessed with two daughters. When Lancaster Colony purchased Fostoria Glass Company in 1986, Jon was still doing design work.

He continued on as a consultant to them for another two years. In 1988, he started his own business called Design Prototypes and was doing freelance work. Jon was hired by Fenton in 1994 to be a product designer and sculptor. Jon felt lucky to be at Fenton where he could design what he had always wanted, sculptured items. Jon has thrived at Fenton and has attracted collectors to his type of work. Even though Jon retired from Fenton in 2004, he is continuing to do work for them.

rounded shape that has a decorative banded design on the lower half. She has also designed another basket for QVC.

Suzi Whitaker, Fenton Art Glass designer

Suzi Whitaker

After graduating from the Art Institute of Pittsburgh, Suzi worked in several areas of Graphic Design and Advertising. In 1994, she started to work for Carson Industries, where she developed her sculpting skills. She fell in love with the medium, but after several years, she left to pursue computer graphics. Suzi came to work at Fenton in March 2003, working part of the time with Jon Saffell. Once he retired, Suzi took over doing the same type of designs. Her favorite medium, like Jon, is clay. She loves taking a clump of clay and magically changing it in an object. Suzi relates, "its like painting, only with clay."

Her most recent challenging project was to redesign the Dancing Lady covered urn from the 1930s. The original moulds were lost during the World War II scrap drive. The new urn is of a new size and shape and the ladies were sculpted to match the originals as closely as possible. Suzi has just designed a new basket for Fenton. It is a small

Wayne King, Fenton Art Glass chemist

Wayne King

Wayne was Fenton's master chemist for many years. He was hired in 1971 to assist both Isaac Willard, who was supervisor of mixing and Subodh Gupta, whose job was in research and development. Later, Wayne became a lab technician. In 1973 after the death of Willard, Wayne became the supervisor of mixing and furnace. With Gupta leaving in 1983, Wayne moved also into research and development. His job is to design new color formulas plus work with old ones. He needs to develop the new colors to match the current decorating trends. It is not an easy job since so many things can affect each resulting color, such as: formula, melting temperature and time, burner condition and the pot itself. Every factor can influence the outcome of the color. The special colors of Blue Burmese and Lotus Mist were perfected by Wayne along with the many trend setting colors such as Rosemilk, that set Fenton apart from other companies. Wayne left Fenton in 2003 to gain experience at another type of glass making company. He returned to Fenton in 2004 to continue his special glass making formulas.

Greg Lang, Fenton Art Glass technologist

Greg Lang

Greg came to work at Fenton in 1992. He was hired to help with the glass formulas and to assist Wayne King. His current job title is Chief Production engineer and Glass Technologist. Greg has a degree in Glass & Ceramic Engineering from Iowa State University. He has 20 years experience in the hand glass industry from Wheaton and Sylvania. He is married and has one son named Seth.

Bob Hill, former mould shop Foreman

Bob Hill

Bob began his work in the glass industry at Wheaton Glass from 1965 to 1967. He was hired by Fenton in 1967 to work at Armstrong Tank Work, a company then owned by Fenton. There he learned to make the fabricating forms used for concrete in making bridges, building roofs, and baseball stadiums. In 1969, Bob began his apprenticeship in the Fenton mould shop and worked all the different phases of making glass moulds. Twenty years later on December 1, 1989 Bob was made supervisor of the mould shop. Bob is in charge of having new moulds made along with keeping current moulds in top form. After extensive use, the moulds will get wear spots or develop some type of damage.

The rest of Bob's family also works at Fenton. His wife Pat is a selector. His daughter Amber works in the Fenton Gift Shop and his son Bob III is a Tour Coordinator.

Bob retired from Fenton on November 5, 2003 due to medical problems. He had been employed at this great company for 37 years and three months. The mould shop is now a joint effort with Jeff Zimmerman being the foreman of the shop and Byron Butts the working foreman. Bob still stays in contact with Jeff, Byron, Nancy, and the design committee and provides input on design and does the mould drawings if needed.

Pat Hill, selector

Pat Hill

Pat began work at Fenton on November 1991. She was hired to work in both the Selecting and Packing Departments. She went back and forth between the two. In 1992, she started working at the lehr full time. Her work schedule would alternate with one week being the day shift and the next week being the night shift.

Starting in 2004, she works only the day shift. Her job as a Selector involves checking for defects. Baskets with defects are discarded and broken in a barrel for recycling. This broken glass is known as cullet and can be used in pots to facilitate the melting of new glass. This cullet is also sold to marble factories.

Pam Dick, Assistant to Frank M. Fenton

Pam Dick

Pam began working at Fenton as a decorator in 1978. Since that time she has had many different job responsibilities. Some of her adventures include the following: working in hot metal, shipping, and the finishing departments. In 1985 she was a tour guide with the Fenton Gift Shop. While working at the gift shop she was introduced to the world of Fenton collectors. Pam has been very involved with the clubs and made many friends. Her current job responsibilities lean toward history and design, two of her favorite things. Pam works for Frank M.

Fenton, in the Museum storage area. Cataloging each piece and creating an inventory database keeps her busy. This is a huge task since it includes special orders, QVC, glass from other companies, and souvenirs from many glass clubs. Besides this, Pam is the assistant to Martha Wright, Fenton's marketing consultant. Pam also speaks at collector group gatherings.

Jennifer Maston, Museum Curator

Jennifer Maston

Jennifer came to work at Fenton in 1988 as the museum curator. Jennifer has a multitude of tasks. One of her main tasks is to maintain the museum and to keep track of where all the glass is located. Some may be taken to be photographed and others borrowed for projects. She is there to be of assistance and to answer questions from collectors there and through emails. All reference books and videos are also sold through the museum. The museum is divided into two sections: Ohio Valley room and Blue Ridge room. The original museum occupies the Ohio Valley room and has glass made up until 1980. The Blue Ridge room, located right across the hall holds glass made after 1980. You may wonder where this name came from. Actually it was Frank M's idea to name it this since Fenton is located on this side of the Blue Ridge Mountains. There are many Diamond Optic pieces from QVC along with other newer items.

The all time favorite colors of museum guests are the yellow Burmese, Cranberry and Milk Glass. The favorite baskets are the Big Cookies, 13" crests and the 12" Hobnail, especially in Ruby.

Decorating Department

The decorating department was restarted in April 1968 with the arrival of Louise Piper. Louise was given the job of developing designs and to train about half a dozen people to duplicate her ideas. Today there are over seventy men and women working on different decorations. The original area for the decorating department was in an unused place in the basement. Later a special area was developed for the decorators that allowed people on the factory tour to watch the decorators at work. The factory tour brought the public in to see how glass was really made. The addition of the decorators enabled people to see from start to finish all the varied steps in getting a decorated piece to the shelf to purchase.

Louise Piper, original decorating department head Archival photo reprinted with permission from the Fenton Art Glass Company.

Louise Piper

Louise began her glass decorating career at Jeannette Shade and Novelty Company. Through Tony Rosena, a designer at Fenton, Louise was hired to set up the new Fenton Decorating Department in 1968. Her first decoration was Violets in the Snow. When the production of Burmese began, she designed the Rose and Scene patterns. Through the years, Louise developed countless decorations. Initially none of her pieces were signed. In later years she began signing her pieces she decorated for collectors in the gift shop. She retired from Fenton in 1989 at the age of 81. She dearly loved her work and that kept her working long past when most people would have retired. Louise passed away in 1995.

Kim Barley, decorator designer. She is shown holding the Black basket with the Blue Hydrangeas decoration she designed.

Kim Barley

Kim came to work at Fenton in 1979 as a decorator. Through the years she has worked to train other decorators. She now has taken on the position to be a designer. Her favorite outdoor scenes involve water and they are frequently part of her designs. Like her colleagues, she has received the

Discovery Award plus others from National Association of Limited Edition Dealer (NALED).

A realistic Blackberry Bouquet basket from 1998 was designed by Kim. Several of her most recent decorations involve Christmas flowers. The Royal Lenton Rose is from 2003 and the Magnolia Blush is from 2004.

Favorite baskets designed by Kim include several different styles. One of them is her first Mary Gregory design. It was done on the #7134SH Spring basket and featured a girl showing a bouquet of flowers to her favorite kitty. This Emerald Green basket done in 2004 is titled appropriately, Bouquet for Kitty. Kim is a big fan of black glass. Kim's design of Blue Hydrangeas was done on black glass and featured a footed basket. She was especially pleased with this combination. Another favorite was a Blue Burmese basket done for QVC. This featured her first water based paint design of pansies.

Kim and her husband Bernie are big fans of Nascar. They have eight children between them. Kim also enjoys collecting items about Elvis, Marilyn Monroe and Princess Diana.

Frances Burton

Frances started her training in 1973 under the watchful eye of Louise Piper. Eventually, Frances moved on to train other new decorators. She became later a designer and then moved into the position of head designer. In 1991 she took over the position of department supervisor. Frances has also received the Discovery award.

Frances is always using different techniques to accent her designs. A memorable recent design was the Wine Country decoration. This featured a beautiful clump of lush grapes on Ruby Amberina Stretch. The collection was developed for the 2003 catalog. A ribbed basket from this collection was featured as part of the Family Signature Series line. Don Fenton's signature was on this basket. With Don's passing in February 2003, it took on added significance since this would be the last piece to bear his name in the regular catalog. Frances also designed the decoration for the first full line

of Burmese in many years. The Let's Bee Burmese was a play on words with a bee flying across the beautiful shades of Burmese.

A favorite basket for Frances was the #6335WS Seasons done in Ruby and featured a little girl with a scarecrow. Frances had been assigned to decorate a ruby basket as part of the Seasons line with a fall theme. The little girl is actually her five year old granddaughter, Savannah Rose. The idea came from visiting a local pumpkin patch with her. Two other favorites were done for QVC. They are #HV50368 in Burmese and #CV0704Q in Cranberry Opalescent. Both of these featured hand painted roses and forget-me-nots, which are both favorite flowers of Frances.

Frances Burton, decorator designer. She is shown holding the Ruby basket with the Fall Seasons decoration she designed.

Robin Spindler, decorator designer. She is shown holding the Topaz Opalescent basket with the Lemonade decoration she designed.

Robin Spindler

Robin's love of art and painting led her to Fenton in 1979 as decorator. Even though her real name is Judith Kay, she goes by Robin but signs all of her pieces "J.K. Spindler." She is grateful everyday to have a job where she can utilize her God given abilities. Her skilled details to all of her designs have lead to several Discovery awards.

One of her designs was a beautiful basket in Burmese featuring a blue bird. This piece was part of the Connoisseur line in 1999 and had twelve Fenton family signatures on it. The Lemonade decoration on Topaz was a Showcase Dealer Exclusive in 2004. A recent Christmas design was a bright white shining star on ruby that was titled Star Bright for 2004.

Stacy Williams, decorator designer. She is shown holding the Cobalt basket with the Mary Gregory decoration called Catch which she designed.

Stacy Williams

Stacy went to school at the Columbus College of Art and Design. In 1993, after graduation, Stacy started work at Fenton as a decorator. She moved up to the position of Designer seven years later. Stacy's artistic talent has really made an impression on all her many designs.

Stacy's favorite basket is the Mary Gregory Winter Seasons basket she designed in Cobalt. The basket is titled Catch, #5977TT. She was expecting at the time and designed the child in it to look like either a boy or girl. Later, she gave birth to a baby boy named Josey. Stacy has nicknamed him, Tadpole. Stacy has a love of frogs as evidenced in several of her designs. The dog in the scene of this same basket is her own dog, Benny, who was a stray that found his way to her home and heart in 2001. Several other Mary Gregory designs that Stacy did were: Vintage Stroke in 2001, Special Treat in 2003 and My First a Pony in 2004. The Dancing Daisies design on Celeste Blue Stretch is also another creation from Stacy.

Stacy lives on her father's farm in Mineral Wells, West Virginia where she and her husband David have built a house.

CC Hardman, decorator designer. She is shown holding the Blue Topaz Overlay Melon basket with the floral decoration she designed.

C.C. Hardman

C.C. began working at Fenton as decorator in 2000. On her six month employee evaluation, Frances asked her to be a lead decorator to assist in training others. She became a trainer and special order designer in March 2003. Three months after taking this new assignment, she was asked to design a QVC piece. From there, her projects have escalated.

C.C. loves the colors and styles of the Victorian era. Scroll work is usually a major part of her designs. Ironically, though she does not decorate her home that way. She loves creating and redesigning the Victorian style for Fenton customers.

Her new designs will be part of the 2005 line. They include: a black vase in the Platinum Collection, a series of designer hats, and a continuation of the Inspirations line from 2004.

Her hobbies involve: photography and road trips to "no where" flea markets. Her life has revolved around art. She took every available art course in high school. A highlight her senior year was creating a post card for the Hospice Foundation. She used the following mediums to create her final image: acrylic, sketching, pen, and ink.

C.C. resides in Mineral Wells, West Virginia with her two sons, Jordon and Coby, along with partner and fellow decorator, Karen Easton.

Martha Reynolds, former decorator designer
Archival photo reprinted with permission from the Fenton Art Glass Company.

Martha Reynolds

Martha came to work for Fenton in 1990. She became one of the Decorating Designers. Through the years, Martha has been honored with many prestigious awards, including the Vandenoever Award from the Society of Glass and Ceramic Decorators, for her very expressive decorations. In 2001, Martha retired from Fenton to start her own designing company.

Chapter 2
Steps of Production

Glass is a unique substance that bears both the qualities of a solid and a liquid. The chemicals used to make glass are simple ingredients but when combined and heated become a new mystical creation. The major ingredients are sand, soda ash, and lime. In addition, a small amount of the following chemicals, when mixed with the main ingredients will help determine a special color. Many times Fenton has other unique ingredients to add but they are trade secrets by them. Several of these colors are also heat sensitive and the final color is determined by reheating.

Alumina & Fluorine = Milk Glass
Cobalt = Blue
Copper = Blue
Gold = Cranberry & Rosalene

Gold & Uranium = Burmese
Chromium = Green
Iron = Green
Iron & table sugar = Amber
Erbium = Pink
Manganese = Black
Neodymium = Pink
Phosphate = Opalescent
Selenium & Cadium = Ruby & Orange
Selenium & Manganese = Crystal
Uranium = Topaz

Once all the ingredients are mixed, they are hand shoveled in a pot in the central furnace. This batch is then heated to about 2500 degrees. This usually takes about 30 hours. The glass is molten at this time and ready to be worked.

Detail of basket, #V51468, shown sitting in front of the cast iron mould used in the production of this piece.

The time needed to make a new mould can take a minimum of two months up to a year depending on when the item is needed for a catalog. The whole process can take from seven to eleven steps. These steps are: design group, master, drawing, foundry, silicone cast, deckle master, milling of joints, duplicating, vise work, lathe work, and assembly. Depending on the piece, there could be eight people involved to do the various steps. Besides the time, the cost of the moulds are very expensive from $500 for a paperweight up to $16,000 for a new animal. On the blown moulds, there is only one made. For the animal figurines, there are four moulds per set.

All the other types of press moulds are made in sets of two. Fenton's mould shop makes most of their own moulds but occasionally a piece can get contracted out to Island Mould to do. Maintenance is an important criteria with the mould cost being so high. If the presser and mould cleaning personnel take proper care of them, the moulds can last for years. Several of the Fenton moulds are from the 1920s and they are still in good working order.

The following steps show the glass from being a molten glob to the final step of emerging as basket. There could be several more steps in addition if the basket is hand painted.

Gather for a blow shop

Blocking the gathered shape

Increasing the size of the blocked shape

Warm in the gather

Blowing into the mould

Mould shaped piece

Snap-up piece and warm it in
the Glory Hole

Wrap colored ring onto top flange

Spray iridescence onto piece

Finisher gets piece after another warming in

Reheating of the future basket in
the Glory Hole before the
crimping is applied.

Flare prior to crimping the flange

Flare prior to crimping the flange

Just entering the crimping tool

Finishing the crimp

Starting the crimp

Finishing the crimp

Finisher shaping the entry flanges to receive the handle ends

Rolling the handle

Entering the ribbed handle mould

Handlers in operation

Shaping the a ribbed handle in the handle mould

Gaffer holding handle and waiting for basket bottom to arrive at handler's chair

Attaching the handle at the "First Stick"

Firmly attaching the handle stick with the handlers marking tool

Finishing up the handle stick

Carry-in to the lehr for annealing

Basket emerging from the lehr, stresses relieved

Chapter 3
Handles

After opening the glass factory in 1905, Frank L. and John Fenton needed employees for their new company. Men and boys from Jefferson Glass were hired.

Each person applying the handles to Fenton baskets, known as a handler, has his own special set of shears. This is a multipurpose tool that allows the handler to cut the stream of glass from the gatherer after the initial piece is first attached to the basket. The remaining piece of glass is then attached to the other side and worked to make the desired arch above the basket. This all takes precise training and skill. At the end of the shears is the mark that is pressed into the glass where it is attached to the basket.

Handlers

Frank Meyers is shown applying a handle to a pitcher. Archival photo reprinted with permission from the Fenton Art Glass Company.

Pete Raymond

Pete was employed at Jefferson Glass before coming to work at Fenton in 1907. 20-year-old Pete Raymond had just received his skilled glass workers card. He was one of the workers to be on the job the first day Fenton operated. Wages at that time were determined by a four and half hour interval called a turn. Glass workers would work two turns a day. Pete, for instance, earned $1.47 a turn at that time. Pete was quick to learn new skills. While the European workers were at Fenton in the 1920s, he learned the many special techniques from them that were unheard of in the glass making business here in the United States. He utilized his new found skills to become a highly valued worker at Fenton. Pete left Fenton in 1913 to work at other glass factories before returning to Fenton in 1921 and stayed there until he retired in 1964. Upon returning, Pete developed more skills on gathering and finishing.

Pete Raymond learned the technique of handling from Frank Meyers in 1939 and became Fenton's second handler. He developed his own special mark and applied it with pride to the handles he put on baskets.

Pete also loved flowers and raised roses. He was a minister in the comunity at the Jehovah Witness Church. Frank M. Fenton shared the following thought. "When Pete Raymond became seventy years old, he was worried about his skills and came to me with the following comment. 'Frank, when you think I'm not pulling my weight, come and let me know so I can decide to retire at that time rather than for you to retire me.'" Frank never had to make this decision; Pete decided on his own at age 78.

Frank Meyers

Frank was a glass worker who had an impact on the early days of Fenton. He learned how to apply handles on baskets at Diamond Glassware Company. While learning this technique at Diamond, he developed his own special mark to apply to the basket to signify that he had put the handle on this basket. This was a mark of prestige to show he was proud of his job.

The importance of the mark continued with Frank Meyers when he joined Fenton in 1932 and until he retired in 1962. Fenton had been making baskets at this time but not with applied handles. Their baskets had metal and wicker handles put on after the basket was made. Applying glass handles was a whole new way of doing things. Finally in 1938, Fenton put baskets with applied handles into production.

Frank's hobby was raising flowers. His great passion was dahlias and he actually developed several new types.

As Fenton's baskets became more popular, more handlers were needed to be trained. It was not a requirement of Fenton at this time for the handlers to mark the basket. Charles Hummel and Johnny Haddix were trained to be handlers but didn't develop a special mark.

The following series of photos are from the Fenton archival library and show the skill of each worker while handling molten glass. Other photos show some of the present-day glass workers.

Don Badgley is applying the handle on the basket. Archival photo reprinted with permission from the Fenton Art Glass Company.

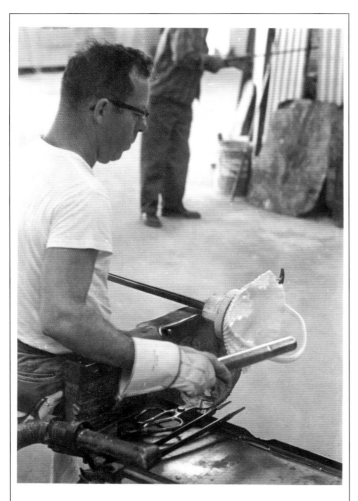

Denzil Austin Dallison, called Pete at the factory, is shaping the handle on a basket. Archival photo reprinted with permission from the Fenton Art Glass Company.

Fred Bruce is attaching the handle to the basket. Archival photo reprinted with permission from the Fenton Art Glass Company.

Ron Bayles is applying a crest to a vase.
Archival photo reprinted with permission
from the Fenton Art Glass Company.

Jr. Thompson is shaping the handle.
Archival photo reprinted with permission from the Fenton Art
Glass Company.

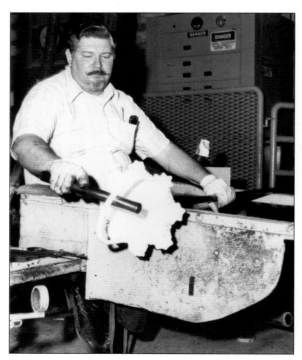

Bob Oliver is shaping the arch of the basket handle.
Archival photo reprinted with permission from the
Fenton Art Glass Company.

Robert Patterson is shaping the handle.
Archival photo reprinted with permission
from the Fenton Art Glass Company.

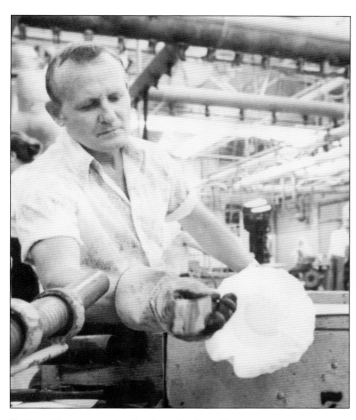

Left: Andy Newland; **Right**: Brian Greene

Delmar Stowasser is shaping the handle.
Archival photo reprinted with permission from the Fenton Art
Glass Company.

Dave Vincent is applying a crest to a vase.
Archival photo reprinted with permission
from the Fenton Art Glass Company.

Left to Right: David L. Vincent; Howard
(Butch) Wright; Jon Anderson

Left: Tom Ingram Jr.; **Right**: James Ralston

Frank Workman

Bob Buchanan

Left to Right: Mike Sine Jr.; Gregg Parsons; Robert (Woody) Patterson

Handler Marks

One of the characteristics of putting on the applied handle is that there was a roughness on the edge. Factory manager Lawrence Badgley ("Badg," as he was known at the factory) had a good working relationship with Frank M. Fenton. His son, Don Badgley, was one of the handlers in the 1950s. Don had noticed that when Frank Meyers and Pete Raymond applied their marks that this helped eliminate the rough spot that occurs when the handle is first applied. He talked to his Dad about this and made the suggestion to have all the handlers utilize marks. Badg took the idea to Frank in about 1953 and said his son made the suggestion that if everyone used a special mark on the basket that would help take care of this roughness. Frank agreed to this and after that, all handlers soon developed their own mark.

All of the men trained to be handlers were also finishers. Many times while on a finishing job, they also could be pulled off at any time to put handles on a basket and then return to their finishing position. Today, the men frequently change jobs. Each man is trained to do several jobs as needed. If someone was listed as a handler today, tomorrow he could be finishing.

Following is a list of marks used by each of the different handlers through the years. Each handler develops his own special mark. Each mark is only used by the handler assigned to it. Notice the uniqueness in each one. Once the handler retires, the mark is also retired. The years given by each handler's name indicate the years of employment at Fenton, not just the years the man was a handler.

Handler mark of Pete Raymond 1905 to 1913 and 1921 to 1964

Handler mark of Pete Dallison 1933 to 1982

Handler mark of Fred (Frank) Bruce 1953 to 1990

Handler mark of Don Badgley 1953 to 1978

Handler mark of Ron Bayles 1956 to 2000

Handler mark of an Apprentice

Handler mark of Frank Meyers 1932 to 1962

Handler mark of Junior Thompson 1957 to 1977 and 1990 to 1993

Handler mark of Edwin Junior Garber 1957 to 1968

Handler mark of Floyd Duff 1962 to 1978
He left to work in a coal mine.

Handler mark of Terry Deuley 1989 to present
Terry is currently not handling.

Handler mark of Bob Buchanan 1990 to present
Bob is now a foreman and is very effective in this job.

Handler mark of Dave Vincent 1964 to present
Dave came to work at Fenton in August 1964 and started work as a gatherer. He is now is one of the lead handlers.

Handler mark of Delmer Stowasser 1965 to 1990

Handler mark of Ronald Farley 1993 to present

Handler mark of Tom Ingram I 1996 to present

Handler mark of Butch Wright 1973 to present

Handler mark of Bob Patterson 1973 to present
Bob had advanced to management and then recently was moved back to being a skilled glass worker.

Handler mark of Robert Camden, presently at Fenton

Handler mark of Andy Newland, presently at Fenton

Robert Oliver 1957 to 1995

Handler mark of Brian Green, 1986 to present

Handler mark of Lloyd Lauderman 1953 to 1993

Handler mark of Tom Ingram II, presently at Fenton

Handler mark of JR Phillips 1986 to 1995

Handler mark of Jim Ralston, presently at Fenton

Handler mark of Gregg Parsons, presently at Fenton

Handler mark of Frank Workman, presently at Fenton

Applying a Handle

The art of applying a handle on a Fenton basket takes a skillful eye. The specialized glass worker whose job is to apply a handle is known as a handler. This job only requires about 30 seconds of pre-cision to take the molten glass, apply it to the basket and then bring its desired shape before the glass cools and hardens. You can imagine how adept you have to be at this job to get the handle attached in such a short period of time.

Typical two handler
setup for a basket shop
Left: Butch Wright;
Right: David Vincent

Handler David Vincent applying "First Stick" to the basket

Ron Bayles is applying a molten ribbon of glass that will become the handle.
Archival photo reprinted with permission from the Fenton Art Glass Company.

Ron Bayles is shaping the handle into an arch.
Archival photo reprinted with permission from the Fenton Art Glass Company.

Handler Butch Wright applying the "First Stick" of the handle to the basket

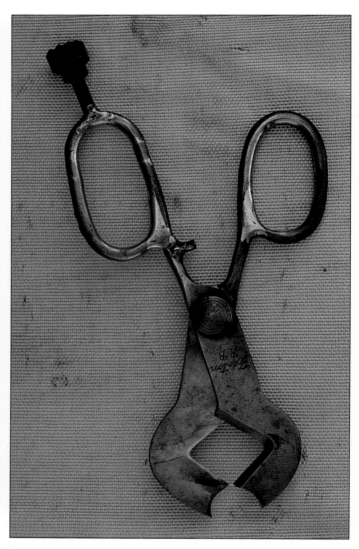

The tool shown here is used to place the particular handlers mark on the end of the basket handle.
Archival photo reprinted with permission from the Fenton Art Glass Company.

Overall view of the cutoff shears with the handler mark on the end

Closeup of the handler mark attached to the shears

Closeup of the handler mark

Types of Handles

Metal

This type of handle was made out of chrome and had a round opening at each end to fit over the knobs on the basket. These handles were not made at Fenton and had to be contracted out. You will find both plain and fancy handles on these baskets. It is our opinion that the plain ones were sold at less expensive discount stores, while the fancy decorated handles would have been sold at more expensive stores.

Wicker

The wicker handle was woven and featured wide loops at each end. These were not made at Fenton but were ordered from another company that made that type of item. To distinguish the original wicker from other ones, they have a black strip that is woven along the top. It is our opinion that Fenton might have ordered them this way to make their handles special from others produced during the same time period. You will find that many Japan cookie jars have a similar wicker handle without the black woven piece.

Glass

In the 1940s, a change was made from having metal or wicker handles put on Fenton baskets to using applied glass handles. There are several different variations of the glass handle. Many times the handle is clear, but other times the handle is colored to match the color of the basket. Sometimes, there could be an opalescent handle. According to Frank M. Fenton, there are several different ways to obtain opalescence on a handle. Since it has taken them years to develop the technique, it is their trade secret.

The Research and Development teams work on developing new types of handles. The Design Department decides which type of handle looks best on a particular basket. The Sales Department or the customer could also have a say, if a special order is being done for them. The decision is always a group decision not made by one particular person.

The following photos show different types of applied handles that Fenton could use on their baskets.

Plain: The glass is applied without any special treatment.

Notched: This handle is also called nicked. After the glass has been applied, the handler takes a tool and leaves notched marks on the glass.

Ribbed: The glass applied to the
basket that has a ribbed effect.

Rope: The handlers puts wide twists in the
glass as it is being applied to the basket.

Twisted Rib: The handler gives the the glass a
slight twist as it is being applied to the basket.

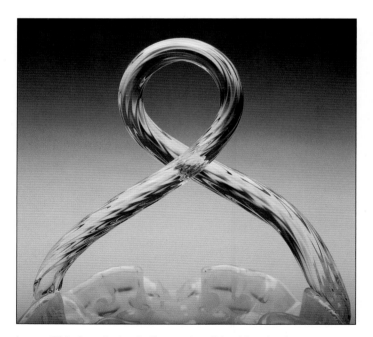

Loop: This handle is similar to the ribbed but in the center
the handler gives the glass an additional twist as it is
being applied to the basket.

Marks of Quality

Each Fenton basket carries an individual handler's mark. **The highly-skilled handler attaches a glowing gob of molten glass to the piece, creates his unique personal "stamp" with a special tool, and fashions a graceful arch!** Thus, each Fenton basket proudly bears the "signature" of the artisan who helped produce it.

Handler's Marks

Bob Buchanan
Ronald Farley
Brian Green

Tom Ingram
Andy Newland
Gregg Parsons

Jim Ralston
Dave Vincent
Frank Workman

Butch Wright
Apprentice Mark

The marks of quality tag is put on basket handles as they are packed at the factory. The tag itself is 2.5" tall and 3.5" wide. Reprinted with permission from the Fenton Art Glass Company.

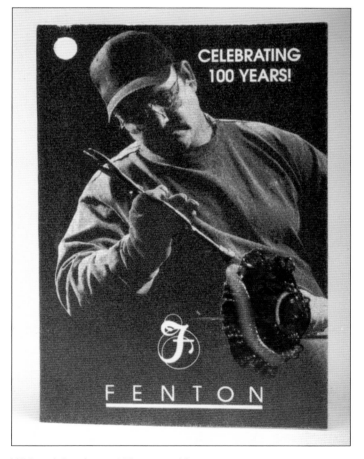

With celebrating a 100 years, this new tag is being put on baskets. Reprinted with permission from the Fenton Art Glass Company.

The Artistry of Cranberry

It takes a team to create Cranberry!

More than 25 Fenton glassworkers comprise the "shop" which makes this exquisite Cranberry basket.

The magic begins when a glassworker (1) called a caser attaches a "bud" of glass containing pure gold to a blowpipe.

Other glassworkers gather crystal over the bud, shape it by "blocking" in soapy water (2), and gently expand the gob (3) before passing the blowpipe to a glassblower.

The glassblower (4) stands on a platform with the mould below his feet.

Note the thin crystal "overblow" (5) on the piece that has just been removed from the mould.

After the overblow is removed, the piece is reheated and taken to the finisher. He skillfully employs a carbon paddle to flare the top (6) and then uses a special device (7) to crimp the piece in preparation for the basket handle.

Elsewhere, a handle gatherer prepares just the right amount of pure crystal (8) to make a perfect handle. Note the ribs imparted to the glass by the mould (9).

The handler attaches the glowing gob (10) of molten glass, marks it at each end with his personal tool, (11) and fashions a graceful arch (12) — all within 25 seconds!

FENTON
Handcrafted American Glass Artistry
www.fentonartglass.com

The display sign, Artistry of Cranberry, is used in the Fenton Gift Shop and retailers across the United States to show the steps of making a basket. Reprinted with permission from the Fenton Art Glass Company.

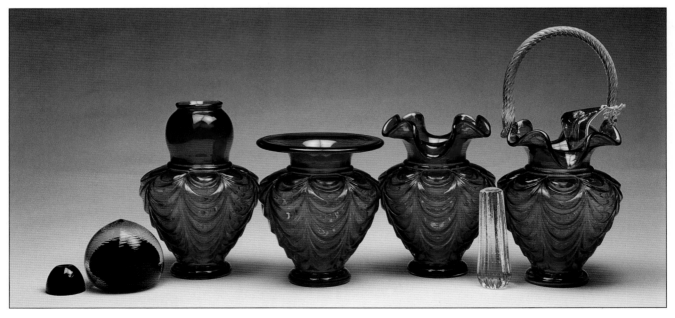

This is a Cranberry progressive set, #PG001CC. It shows the different stages of making a basket.
Left to Right: Ruby gold, cased ruby gold block, unfinished vase, finished vase, crimped vase, ribbed crystal gather for handle, finished basket

artful celebration

*Cranberry glass is made
in the USA exclusively by Fenton*

𝓕 F E N T O N

Handcrafted American Glass Artistry

For more information call 1-800-933-6866 or visit our web site at www.fentonartglass.com

The Sign, Artful Celebration, shows the finished basket.
Reprinted with permission from the Fenton Art Glass Company.

Chapter 4
Channels of Distribution

Baskets were produced at Fenton in the following different categories.

General catalog: Each item listed this way was a regularly produced piece that was generally available for the entire year.

Spring Supplement: This item was produced for a short period of time, usually from January until April or May. The item may also be a numbered limited edition or just made for this time frame.

Connoisseur: For the June supplement, there were special items made, usually a type of art glass. This type of collection debuted in 1983. The artists were given the opportunity to develop unique items of interest to collectors. New techniques were sometimes tried for this collection. These items were usually numbered and/or were all made in limited edition.

Centennial Collection: This collection was begun in 2000 to celebrate the countdown to the 100th anniversary in 2005. The idea was to highlight favorite types of glass by the various family members. Each year, two family members would select their favorite type of glass. Each piece would be signed by that person.

Showcase Dealer Exclusives: Certain Fenton retailers were given the status of being a showcase dealer by having a high volume of sales. This program was begun in 1994 to reward these dealers. For these elite dealers, a special exclusive piece was made to encourage collectors to come into their stores.

Catalog Exclusive: In the early 1990s, a smaller version of the general catalog was made available. These small catalogs have the store name printed on them and could be mailed to their mail order customers. In 1995, a new program was started for those retailers that used this catalog. Limited edition pieces were featured in the catalog that could be ordered only through the store listed on the catalog.

Glass Messenger Exclusive: With all the glass they were producing, Fenton decided they should have their own publication to highlight their glass, artists, decorators, family members, and special stories. The Glass Messenger made its debut in early 1996. Each subscriber to the quarterly newsletter was given a certificate for the opportunity to purchase an exclusive piece of Fenton glass. The piece was made of an unique type of glass. Lynn Fenton Erb was in charge of this publication. Later, responsibility for the Glass Messenger was transferred to Jim Measell, who is now editor.

Showroom Exclusive: In each area of the United States, there are gift showrooms for retail shop owners to visit to actually look at the merchandise first hand. Special pieces were made for shop owners that visited the showroom.

Fenton Gift Shop: There is a gift shop on site that carries first quality merchandise, seconds, overruns, and short runs. Some of the pieces may have a slight blemish on them that are deemed not perfect for the catalog, but put in the gift shop as a second. Sometimes if pieces are being decorated for the regular line, some may be left after the decorating department is done, so the rest of the plain pieces get put in the gift shop for sale. Also if they have glass in the pot that they haven't finished using, then a mould or two may get pulled out to use up the rest of the glass. Each year for the annual February sale, special pieces are made. In June each year, a tent sale is held to clean out overruns and the last year's merchandise. As an additional attraction special pieces are also made for this sale. In August, the Fenton Art Glass Collectors of America have a convention. Since it is held in Williamstown, Fenton makes special edition pieces for convention attendees. These items are put in a Special Glass Room and a lottery is held to determine who goes in the room first. It is like a treasure hunt and after each group goes in additional pieces are added.

QVC Show: This home shopping network was conceived in 1986. Joe Segel, the founder, formerly worked for Franklin Mint. He was responsible for vaulting them to their successful collectible market. QVC stands for Quality, Value and Convenience. In the mid 1980s, Fenton was looking for ways to expose Fenton glass to a new consumer. Shelley Fenton had previously worked with Whitney Smith, head of new products at Franklin Mint. Whitney left Franklin Mint and soon began to work with QVC on obtaining new collectibles for their programs. Because of her past association with Shelley, Whitney thought Fenton would be a good fit with QVC. Several discussions took place with various types of glassware viewed before it was decided to offer Fenton glass on QVC. The very first item was the birthstone bear. At first in 1988, the items on QVC were from Fenton's general catalog. After a few shows, everyone agreed that to be really successful, the Fenton glass items needed to be made exclusively for QVC. The idea was to develop special pieces for this program. Bill Fenton became the main spokesman to talk about Fenton on these select shows. Generally there are about six to eight Fenton programs a year with about a dozen different types of items per show.

Special Orders: Besides producing glass for themselves, Fenton does make special pieces for individuals, companies, and collector groups. A wide range of items have been made through the years. When a special order is placed, Fenton generally requires the order to be a turn. This term applies to the amount of glass that can be made in four hours. A small mould will produce many items while a larger mould will of course result in fewer pieces.

Chapter 5
Designs and Patterns

At age 26, Frank L. Fenton, started his glass company. Previously, he had worked for four different glass companies: Indiana, Jefferson, Bastow and Northwood. Frank was the one primarily responsible for the design of Fenton products until his death in 1948. While he had no formal art training, his ideas came from nature, works of art and even his competitors. When Fenton first started, blanks were bought from Northwood Glass in Wheeling, West Virginia and other glass companies on which to decorate. After Fenton progressed from just being a decorating company to a glass producer, more ideas were needed to develop glass shapes. The first ones naturally came from competitors. Frank always kept in mind the need to be aware of what the public wanted. Staying on top of colors and trends, help keep Fenton in business then and continue to do so today.

After their father's death in 1948, Frank M. and Bill Fenton were thrust with the responsibility of running the company. Since neither had training in design, someone had to come up with ideas. At the time, reproductions of older items were selling quite well. Frank M. Fenton said "We felt that since I was the neophyte, not really very knowledgeable about Early American and Victorian Glass, that I should tour antique shops and antique shows and try to get some ideas for things we might do. I spent a lot of time traveling to learn what was out there in the antique market and when I saw a piece or a design

or a pattern or a handle that I liked, I just bought the piece and brought it back with me. Many of the pieces we made in the 1950s were inspired by old moulds or old shapes that I had acquired at an antique show somewhere."

So where do the ideas for glass patterns come from? At the Corning Museum, in October 1992, Frank M. Fenton gave a seminar about Fenton design and their designers. There he said, "Glass design includes not only pattern, texture and shape, but also color, which is very much a part of the design. I once heard a designer say that there is nothing new under the sun. Of course, he was only partly right. A great deal of our design today and yesterday came from taking something that was made yesterday or 2000 years ago and adapting it to today's needs and tastes."

What Frank M. Fenton conveys is that, like yesterday, all of today's ideas reflect many things. Maybe an old design is used and then adapted to make a new shape, or a single part of a design could be used in combination with something else to develop a new piece. The main considerations are eye appeal and how the piece will react in different colors; it may look good in one color but not in another.

The following patterns, in alphabetical order, were used on Fenton baskets. Photographs of examples are shown after each pattern description.

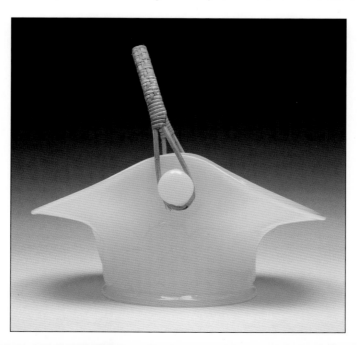

Acanthus

After Imperial Glass Company closed in 1983, Frank M. Fenton went up to Bellaire, Ohio to buy several of their moulds. The Acanthus mould was one he really wanted. He had seen several pieces in antique shops and knew it was a beautiful mould. On the first and second trips, he looked for this mould in particular, but it never materialized. On the third trip, George went with him and helped look.

While searching through the moulds, George managed to find it on a bottom shelf. On that particular trip, a total of 65 moulds were purchased. Since they had purchased many moulds before, they were given a super price of $50 each for the moulds. While getting those moulds, a crate of 30 to 40 spot and optic moulds were offered for sale at $200 and of course Frank took them too.

Acanthus, #9738NK, Cobalt Marigold, 9.5" tall, 9" wide, General Catalog 1987, **$65**

Aurora

Frank M. Fenton has related that the "United States Glass Company made some pieces in a color called Aurora. We named the pattern Aurora mistakenly. It was actually U. S. Glass #310 and that pattern inspired our Aurora pattern."

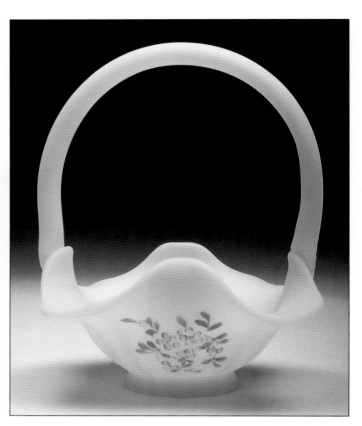

Aurora, #7430, Opal satin, Hand painted flowers, 7.25" tall, 6.5" wide, Fenton Gift Shop, 1991, **$40**

Aurora, #7630KP, Black, Copper Rose decoration, 6.25" tall, 6.25" wide, General Catalog, 1989 to 1993, **$48**

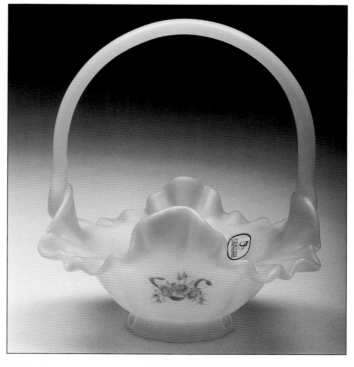

Aurora, #7630AF, Opal gloss, 7" tall, 6.5" wide, Antique Rose decoration, General Catalog 1989, **$45**

Barred Oval

This was an original United States Glass Company pattern from 1891. It was made by George Duncan & Sons division also called Factory D site. Frank M. Fenton purchased a piece of this pattern and had Tony Rosena design new moulds. A whole line of different shapes were designed from the one piece.

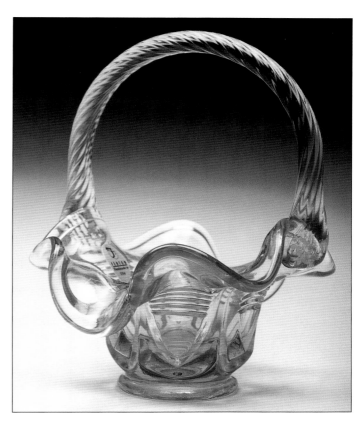

Barred Oval, #8339LC, Ice Blue, 5.5" tall, 4.75" wide, General Catalog 1999, **$30**

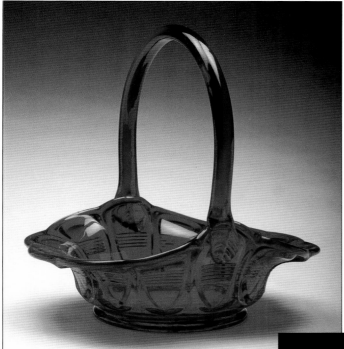

Barred Oval, #8331RU, Ruby, 7.5" tall, 7.5" wide, General Catalog 1985 to 1988, **$48**

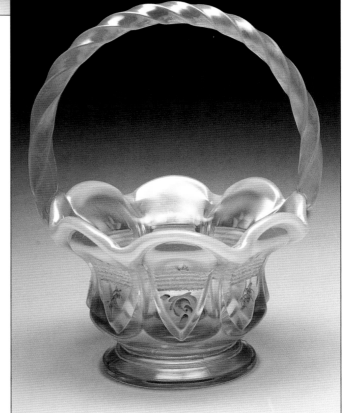

Barred Oval, #CV1586K, Iridized Champayne satin, 8" tall, 6" wide, Hand painted floral, Frank M. Fenton signature, Made for QVC, January 1997, **$42**

Barred Oval, #CV158O9, Spruce Green Carnival, 8" tall, 6" wide, Hand painted with white iced and pink floral, Made for QVC, October 1997, **$45**

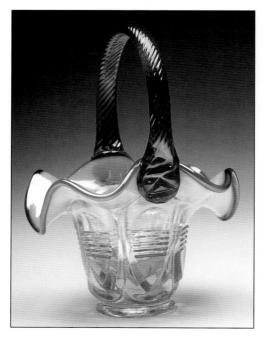

Barred Oval, #C8339EU, Iridized Willow Green Opalescent with cobalt crest & handle, 5.5" tall, 4.75" wide, Made for QVC.com, November 2001, **$45**

Basketweave

Tony Rosena designed this pattern for use at Fenton.

Basketweave, #9335DV, Milk Glass, 7.2" tall, 5.8" wide, Violets in the Snow decoration, General Catalog 1979 to 1980, **$85**

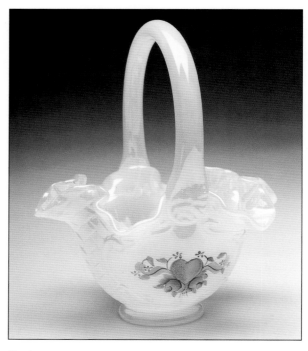

Basketweave, #9335FH, Iridized Milk Glass, 7" tall, 5.75" wide, Hearts and Flowers decoration, General Catalog 1990 to 1991, **$38**

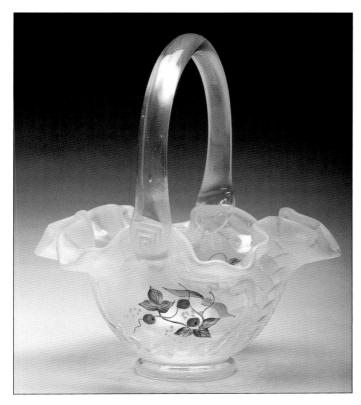

Basketweave, #9335SB, Iridized French Opalescent, 7" tall, 6.25" wide, Snowberry decoration, Christmas Supplement 1992, **$45**

Basketweave with open edge

An early Fenton pattern that was first used with carnival glass. This pattern is very popular with collectors with its delicate open lace edge. The edge is also where the damage easily occurs due to the thinness of the glass. Carefully examine your piece to make sure there isn't any cracks or chips.

Basketweave with Open Edge, #8335OO, Provincial Blue, 7.2" tall, 6" wide, General Catalog 1987 to 1988, **$45**

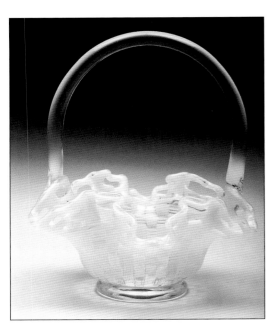

Basketweave with open edge, #8335UO, Peaches' n Cream, 7" tall, 6.5" wide, General Catalog 1987 to 1988, **$45**

Basketweave with Open Edge, #C8335OI, Teal Marigold, 7" tall, 6" wide, General Catalog 1988, **$38**

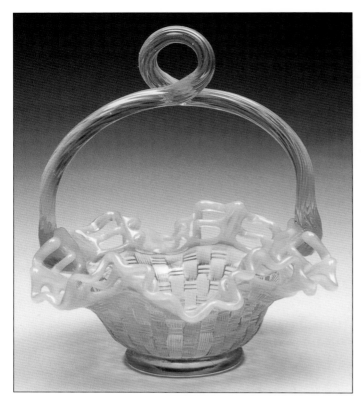

Basketweave with Open Edge, #8335XC, Persian Blue Opalescent, loop handle, 7" tall, 6.76" wide, Collectors Extravaganza Supplement 1989, **$55**

Basketweave with open edge, 7" tall, Made for QVC
Top: #C8335TZ, Twilight Blue Iridized, January 1992, **$35**; **Bottom Left**: #C8335CV, Empress Rose Iridized, October 1998, **$38**; **Bottom Right**: #C8335IO, Stiegel Blue Opalescent, June 1991, **$40**
Note: Empress Rose is a dichroic color and turns a somewhat different color when photographed. It is actually a pink color.

Basketweave with Open Edge, #C8335IP, Plum Opalescent Carnival, 6.5" tall, 5.5" wide, Made for QVC, March 1998, **$48**

Basketweave with open edge, 7" tall, Made for QVC
Top: C8335XB, Black Carnival, April 1990, **$50**; **Bottom Left:** #C8335AI, Aquamarine Iridized, April 2000, **$40**; **Bottom Right:** #C8335SI, Spruce Green Carnival, April 1995, **$40**

Beaded Melon

This pattern was developed at Fenton. The basic pattern started as the #192 Melon. In the 1950s, Frank and Bill were looking for something different to do. They decided to add beads to the melon pattern. It sold well at the time and continues to sell today but it is not one of Frank's favorite ideas. He wishes they hadn't changed the mould.

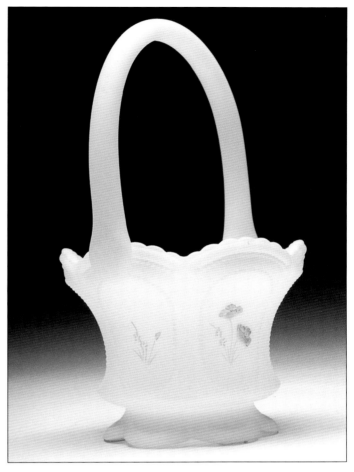

Beaded Panel, #9639JU, Opal satin, 8″ tall, 4.5″ wide, Meadow Blossoms decoration, General Catalog 1986 to 1987, **$58**

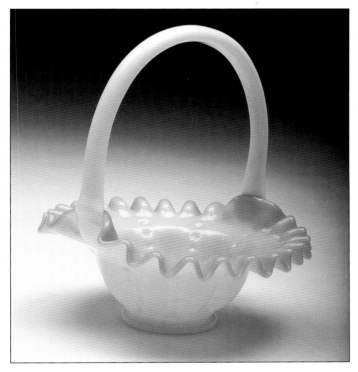

Beaded Melon, #711, Green Overlay, 7.5″ tall, 6.5″ wide, General Catalog 1950, **$95**

Beaded Panel

Beaded Panel is similar to two early pressed glass patterns. A pattern known as Heavy Jewell was made by Fostoria Glass around 1900. The top row of this pattern resembles Fenton's pattern There is another pattern known as Erie or Beaded Ovals in the Sand made by Dugan Glass that also resembles Fenton's pattern. Frank M. Fenton found a sugar bowl in this pattern. A new mould was made at Fenton. Initially the pattern was called Paneled, and later renamed Beaded Panel.

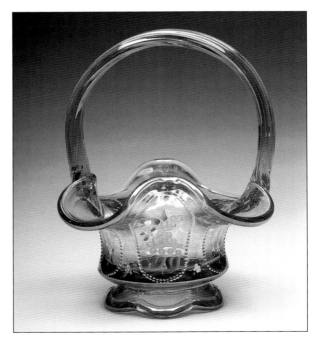

Beaded Panel, #CV1171K, Dusty Rose Iridized, 7″ tall, 6″ wide, hand painted floral, Made for QVC, November 1996, **$45**

Big Cookies

Frank L. Fenton designed this pattern. He frequently went to Atlantic City for wage conferences. One of his favorite things to bring home was saltwater taffy or macaroons. The macaroon cookies became the inspiration for the Big Cookies pattern. It is not known, though, who gave the name to the pattern.

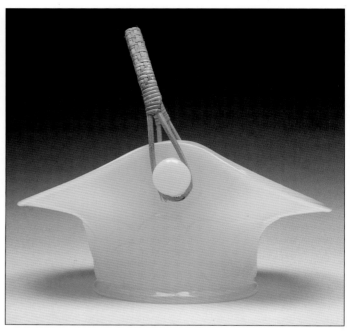

Beaded Panel, #CV117ZQ, Iridized Plum, 7" tall, 6" wide, hand painted with pansies, Made for QVC, August 1997, **$49**

Big Cookies, #1681, with wicker handle, Chinese Yellow, 4.8" tall, 11.5" wide, General Catalog 1932, **$295**

Beaded Panel, 7" tall, 6" wide, Made for QVC **Left:** #CV0359T, Twilight Blue Carnival, Hand painted with pink flowers, June 1993, **$42**; **Right:** #CV035L6, Cape Cod Green Carnival; Hand painted with white floral; October 1995, **$42**

Big Cookies, #1681 with wicker handle, Ruby, 4.8" tall, 11.5" wide, General Catalog 1933, **$250**

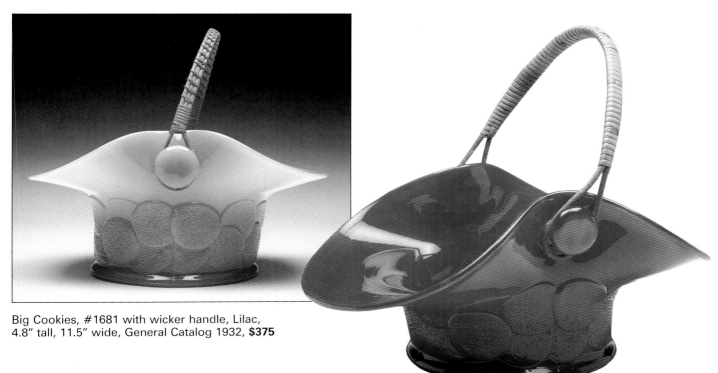

Big Cookies, #1681 with wicker handle, Lilac,
4.8" tall, 11.5" wide, General Catalog 1932, **$375**

Big Cookies, #1681, Mandarin Red, 5.25" tall, 11" wide, with
wicker handle, General Catalog 1933, **$250**

Bubble Optic

This special optic mould was developed at
Fenton. It appears that there are small bubbles on
the surface to make this unique pattern. Imagine a
small child blowing bubbles and having them adhere to the glass surface.

Big Cookies, #1681 with wicker handle, Jade,
5.25" tall, 10" wide, General Catalog 1933, **$195**

Bubble Optic, #1330TE,
Country Cranberry, 7.5" tall, 7"
wide, Hand painted with roses,
Limited to 2500, Connoisseur
Supplement 1989, **$85**

Butterfly & Berry

This pattern was designed by Frank L. Fenton. It is assumed that on one of Frank's many trips, he saw something with this design on it and liked it well enough to have several pieces made. It worked very well with the original carnival glass treatment.

Butterfly & Berry, #9134FO, French Opalescent, 6.25" tall, 4.75" wide, General Catalog, 1986 to 1987, **$38**

Butterfly & Berry, #9134FB, Federal Blue, 7" tall, 4.75" wide, General Catalog 1983 to 1984, **$28**

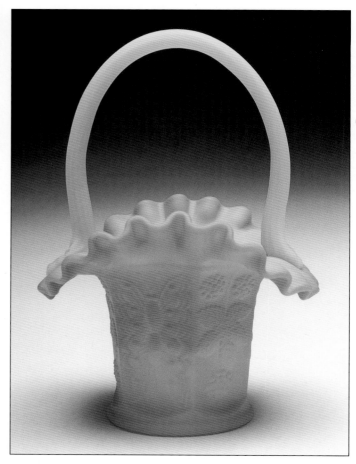

Butterfly & Berry, #9234BR, Burmese, 6.75" tall, 4.25" wide, General Catalog 1986, **$110**

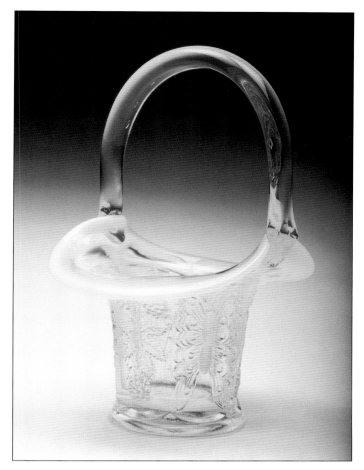

Butterfly & Berry, #9134TO, Topaz Opalescent, 7" tall, 5" wide, Collectors Extravaganza Supplement 1988, **$68**

Butterfly & Berry, #C9134GZ, Green Carnival, 7" tall, 5" wide, Made for QVC, October 1990, **$36**

Butterfly & Berry, #C9134DN, Dusty Rose Iridized with milk glass crest & handle, 7" tall, 5.5" wide, WC Fenton signature, Made for QVC, January 1990, **$55**

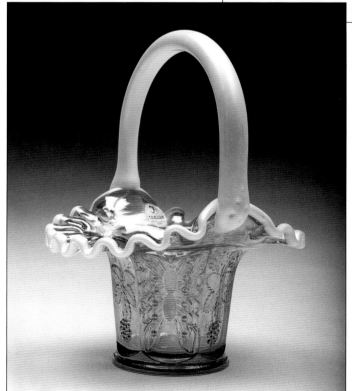

Butterfly & Berry, C9134FD, French Opalescent iridized with Dusty Rose crest and handle, 7.5" tall, 5.25" wide, Made for QVC, June 1996, **$40**

Butterfly & Berry, 7" tall, 5.5" wide, Made for QVC
Top Left: #C9134DN, Dusty Rose Iridized, Teal crest and loop handle, Bill Fenton signature, January 1990, **$65**; **Top Center**: #CV0502K, Plum Carnival, Milk Glass crest, March 1994, **$50**; **Top Right**: #C9134UY, Willow Green Opalescent, Hand painted accents, Black crest, Museum collection, December 2002, **$65**;
Bottom Left: #C91347Q, French Opalescent, Hand painted accents with Cobalt crest and handle, Museum Collection, December 2001, **$60**;
Bottom Right: #C9134OM, Teal Marigold, Milk Glass crest, January 1988, **$55**

Butterfly Net

Fenton developed some stemware with a butterfly net design in the 1930s,. The Fenton Art Glass Collectors of America (FAGCA) have as their logo a butterfly. Their newsletter is called *Caught in the Butterfly Net*. This basket was developed for them.

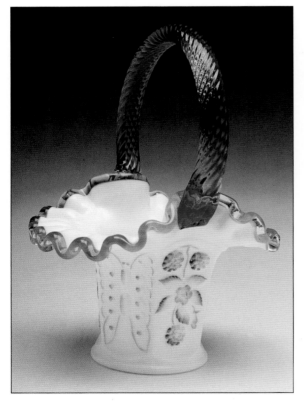

Butterfly & Berry, #C9134G8, Milk glass, Hand painted accents on berries and leaves, Spruce Green crest and handle, 7.25" tall, 5.25" wide, Made for QVC, January 1998, **$49**

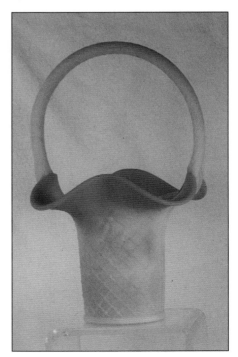

Butterfly Net, Blue Burmese, Made for Fenton Art Glass Collectors of America (FAGCA), 1999, **$48**

Button & Arch

It is assumed that this is an old Duncan pattern. The moulds were acquired from Rolston Westlake, a former Columbus mayor. The man had been in business to have moulds made or reproduced. In the 1950s he would have Fenton make the glass for him and then he would decorate those pieces for fairs or special events. A date or initials of the event and the customers name could be engraved on the piece. After he closed his business, Fenton purchased the moulds.

Button & Arch, 7.5" tall, 5" wide, Made for QVC
Left: #C4637OU, Violet Iridized, Milk Glass crest, February 2003, **$40**; **Center:** #C2734TZ, Twilight Blue Carnival, June 1994, **$28**; **Right:** #C4637O5, Apple Green Iridized, Cobalt crest and handle, December 2003, **$38**

Cactus

The Indiana Goblet and Tumbler Company in Greentown, Indiana, produced the Cactus pattern from 1901 to 1903. This company is often referred to by collectors today as Greentown Glass. Several old pieces of this pattern were purchased and Fenton first reproduced the pattern in the 1950s.

Button & Arch, #4637IP, Plum Carnival, 7.5" tall, 5" wide, Family signing event, 1997, **$49**

Cactus, Topaz Opalescent, General Catalog 1960
Left: #3439TO, 9" tall, **$200**; **Right:** #3437TO, 7" tall, **$125**

Caprice

The Cambridge Glass Company, of Cambridge, Ohio, produced a whole line of this pattern from 1930 to 1957. After Cambridge closed, Imperial Glass Company, of Bellaire, Ohio, acquired some moulds. With the closure of Imperial in 1982, Frank M. Fenton took several trips to Bellaire, Ohio, to acquire some moulds. He purchased one Caprice mould. Several changes were made to the mould to improve the design and distinguish it from the original piece.

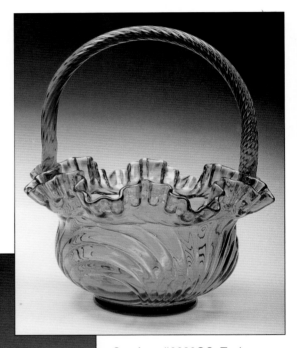

Cactus, #3434RN, Red Carnival, 10" tall 6" wide, Made for Levay, 1982, **$175**

Caprice, #9230OC, Teal Royale, 9.25" tall, 8.5" wide, General Catalog 1988, **$55**

Cactus, #C3436L9, Ice Blue Iridized, 9.25" tall, 6.8" wide, loop handle, Made for QVC, June 2000, **$98**

Caprice, #9732CC, Country Cranberry, 7.25" tall, 4" wide, General Catalog, 1987 to 1990, **$58**

Carolina Dogwood, #2936RC, Red Carnival, 8.5" tall, 10" wide, Damask Rose Decoration designed by Frances Burton, General Catalog 1996, **$85**

Carolina Dogwood

The Westmorland Glass Company made a pattern called Carolina Dogwood in early carnival glass. The Carolina Dogwood was an inspiration to Fenton and a new pattern was created, based on that early pattern.

Carolina Dogwood, #CV089PX, Plum Iridized, 8" tall, Made for QVC, April 1995, **$60**

Carolina Dogwood, #2936CQ, Amethyst carnival, 8" tall, 7.5" wide, White Blossoms, decoration designed by Robin Spindler, General Catalog 2002, **$68**

Chessie, #9480DK, Dusty Rose, 8.5" tall, 7.1" wide, Fenton Gift Shop, 1991, $**295**

Chessie

The Chesapeake and Ohio Railroad started in 1836 and served the needs of many companies and public. As part of their early advertising, a sleeping kitten was designed. This was used for many years that to travel on their trains was like the ease of sleeping like a kitten. This kitten was named, appropriately, Chessie. In the 1960s, this company came to Fenton for them to design a special item as a corporate gift. Tony Rosena came up with a covered candy box with a sleeping kitten. On two separate occasions, this candy box has been used to make a basket. The first time, was in 1997. An iridized Dusty Rose candy box was made for QVC. A few of the candy bottoms were made into baskets to sell in the special glass room at the Fenton Art Glass Collectors of America (FAGCA) convention. In 2003, a special run was done in Red Carnival for the Gillian Collection. For more information about Fenton cats and the Chessie pattern, please refer to our daughter's book, *Fenton Cats and Dogs*, by Tara Coe-McRitche.

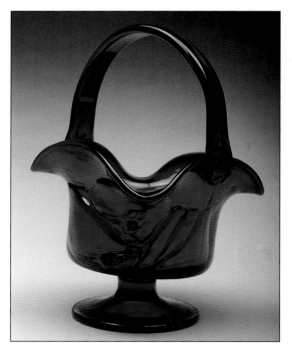

Chessie, #9480RU, Ruby, 8.5" tall, 7.1" wide, Made for David Leo of Jillian Collectibles, 2003, Sample #5 of 8, **$350**

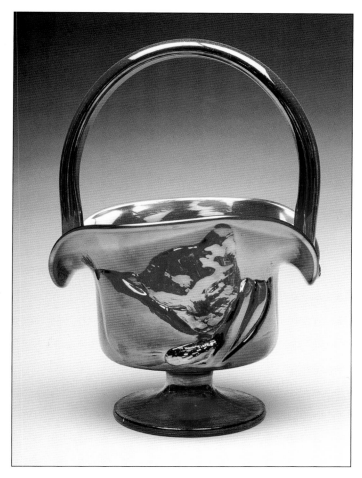

Chessie, #9480RN, Red Carnival, 8.5" tall, 7.1" wide, Made for David Leo of Jillian Collectibles, 2003, **$145**

Coin Dot, #1435XC, Persian Blue Opalescent, 6.5" tall, 4.5" wide, Collectors Extravaganza Supplement 1989, **$40**

Coin Dot

In the early 1910s, several glass companies were making this pattern. The version used by Buckeye Glass in Martin's Ferry most closely matches the Fenton design. Their pattern was called Big Windows. Frank L. Fenton developed the Fenton shapes and then used the Coin Dot spot mould so a contrasting color could be developed in opalescent glass. This pattern is sometimes mixed up with Coin Spot. You can see through the dots on Coin Dot, while on Coin Spot the spots are opalescent and you can't see through them.

Coin Dot, #1435BO, Blue Opalescent, 6.5" tall 4.5" wide, General Catalog 1948-1955, **$78**

Coin Dot, #C1435KO, Cobalt Blue Opalescent, 6.5" tall, 4.75" wide, Frank M. Fenton signature, Made for QVC, January 1996, **$65**

Coin Dot, #DS503T3, Topaz Opalescent, 8.25" tall, 6" wide, Cobalt handle, Made for Westmoreland Museum Gift Shop, 2002, **$68**

Coin Dot, #2435NZ, Rosemilk, 8.25" tall, 6" wide, General Catalog 2003, **$58** **Note:** Rosemilk is a dichroic glass that turns a different color under different lighting, such as when photographed. It is actually an intense pink color. When this basket appeared in the Fenton catalog, the photograph was retouched to create the pink color.

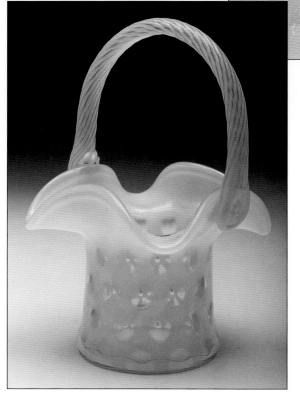

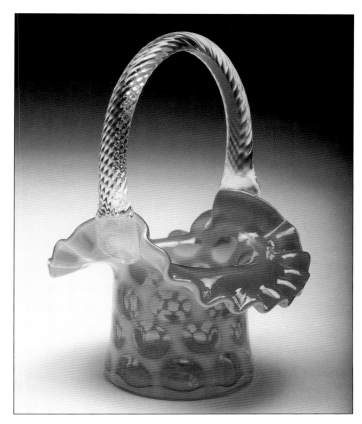

Coin Dot, #DS503CR, Cranberry Opalescent, 6.75" tall 5" wide, Made for Westmoreland Museum Gift Shop, 2004, **$85**

Coin Dot, #203, Honey Suckle, 7.25" tall, 7" wide, General Catalog 1949, **$125**

Coin Dot, #1437CR, Cranberry Opalescent, 7.25" tall, 7.25" wide, General Catalog 1947 to 1965, **$110**

Coin Dot, #1437LO, Lime Opalescent, 7.25" tall, 7.25" wide, 1952 to 1954, **$275**

Coin Dot, #1437TO, Topaz Opalescent, 7.75" tall,
6.75" wide, General Catalog 1959 to 1960, **$150**

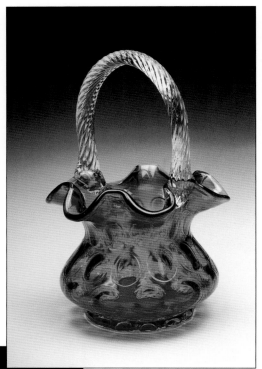

Coin Dot, #1434CC, Country
Cranberry, 8.25" T, 5.5"W,
General Catalog 1983 to
1999, **$50**

Coin Dot, French Opalescent
Top: #1435FO, 5" tall, 4.75" wide, General Catalog 1948 to 1953, **$40**
Bottom Left: #1437FO, 7.25" tall, 7.25" wide, 1947 to 1953, **$55;**
Bottom Right: #1925FO, 10" tall, 6" wide, 1948 to 1951, **$135**

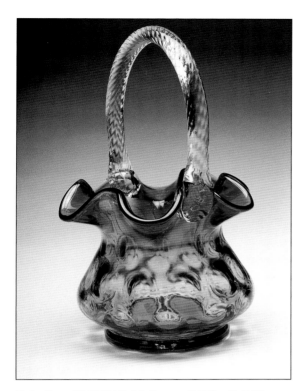

Coin Dot, #1434MG, Mulberry, 8.25" tall, 5.5" wide, General Catalog 1989 to 1992, **$68**

Coin Dot, #1434, Mulberry Opalescent, 7.75" tall, 5.25" wide, Made for Fenton Art Glass Collectors of America (FAGCA), 1989, **$89**

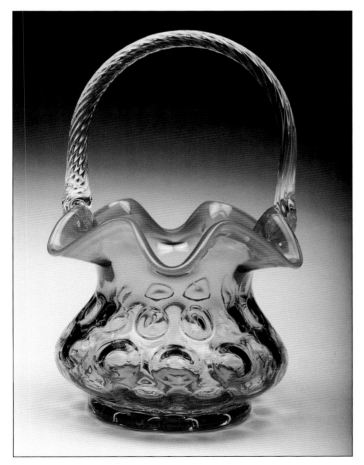

Coin Dot, #1434, Mulberry Opalescent, 7.75" tall, 5.25" wide, Fenton Gift Shop 1992, **$75**

Coin Dot, #1430FO, French Opalescent, 10" tall, 10" wide, General Catalog 1947 to 1951, **$150**

Coin Dot, Cranberry Opalescent
Left: #1353CR, 14" tall, 12" wide, 1947 to 1950, **$500; Right:** #1430CR, 10" tall, 10" wide, 1947 to 1954, **$275**

Coin Spot

A close cousin to the Coin Dot pattern and based on the early 20th century pattern. Many glass houses produced the Coin Spot pattern like Jefferson and Northwood. This pattern is some times mixed up with Coin Dot. You can't see through the spots on Coin Spot, because the spots are opalescent. However, on Coin Dot you can see through the dots.

Coin Spot, #AS644CR Cranberry Opalescent, 13" tall, 8.5" wide, Made for Westmoreland Museum Gift Shop, 2003, **$250**

Coin Spot, #2437TO, Topaz Opalescent, 7" tall, 6.5" wide, Made for Levay, 1977 **$125**

Colonial

This was a pattern from the Westmoreland Glass Company, located in Grapeville, Pennsylvania. This wide panel design was used by different glass companies in the early 1900s. The glass companies of Buckeye, Cambridge, Heisey, and Jefferson all had versions of the Colonial pattern.

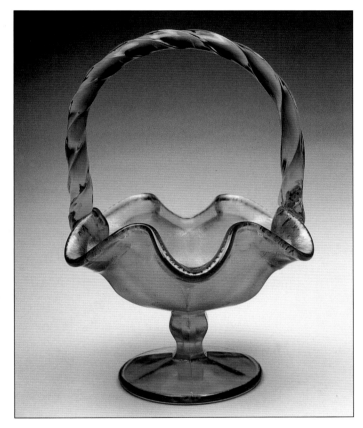

Colonial, #5555SS, Stiegel Green Stretch, 7" tall, 5" wide, Historic Collection, General Catalog 1994, **$60**

Cornshuck or Wheat

While on vacation at a ranch in Colorado, Frank M. Fenton heard about an antique show going on in Denver. Wanting to see what it offered, he hitched a ride on a cattle truck so he could go to the show. While there, he saw a Czechoslovakian vase that resembled bundled wheat and purchased it. He took the vase back home and had the mould shop develop a mould from it. This pattern is sometimes referred to as Wheat by collectors.

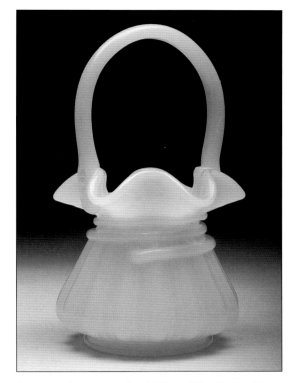

Cornshuck, #5838, Opal Gloss, 7" tall, 4" wide, Fenton Gift Shop 1984, **$30**

Cornshuck, #5838PF, Opal Gloss, 7" tall, 4" wide, Petit Fleur decoration, General Catalog 1984, **$50**

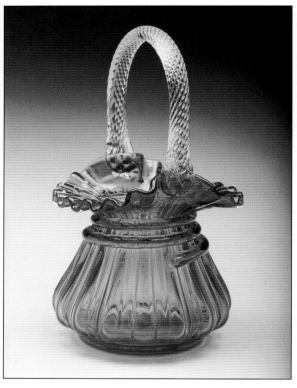

Cornshuck, #5838CC, Country Cranberry, 7" tall, 4" wide, Fenton Gift Shop, 1987, **$60**

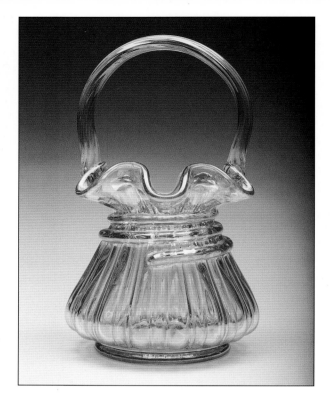

Cornshuck, #C5838LU, Lilac Iridized, 7" tall, 4" wide, Made for QVC, January 1990, **$55**

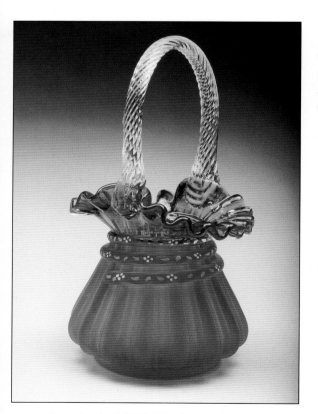

Cornshuck, #Q5838P9, Country Cranberry, 7" tall, 4" wide, hand painted white daisies, Made for Gracious Touch, 1987, **$85**

Crackle

Crackle glass is a special technique of taking hot glass and immersing it in cold water to cause it to crack all over. It is cased with another layer of glass and then reheated to seal all the glass together. The Rainbow Glass Company and Pilgrim and Kanawha Glass both used this type of glass extensively.

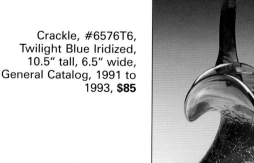

Crackle, #6576T6, Twilight Blue Iridized, 10.5" tall, 6.5" wide, General Catalog, 1991 to 1993, **$85**

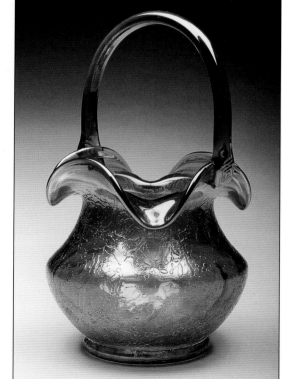

Crests

The art of applying a thin stream of molten glass to the edge of a piece is known as ringing. The glass worker doing this job is known as a ringer. He has to be very skilled to achieve a uniform thickness as the glass is spun around. After this special edge has been applied, it is reheated to allow the glass to adhere to each other. The next step is to pass the piece off to the finisher to flare out the edge or to give it a crimp. Glass with this ribbon of glass was known to be crested or petticoat glass. It is our opinion that the idea for this decoration was inspired by the central European glass artisans of the 1920s. Crests have become a trademark of Fenton. Many different colors have been used.

Pete Raymond first learned this ringing skill in the 1930s. He wondered if a colored glass could be applied to a French Opalescent piece. Cobalt glass was spun on French Opalescent and Fenton's first crest line of Blue Ridge was introduced in 1939.

For a complete listing of Aqua, Emerald, and Silver crest patterns, please refer to our book, *Elegant Glass: Early, Depression and Beyond.*

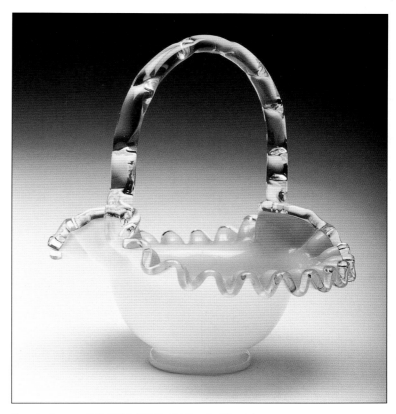

Peach Crest, #7237PC (203), 7.5" tall, 7" wide, General Catalog 1940 to 1949, **$75**

Silver Turquoise, #7237ST, 8" tall, 6.5" wide, General Catalog 1956, **$68**

Ivory Crest, #1923, 7.5" tall, 7" wide, General Catalog 1941 to 1942, **$95**

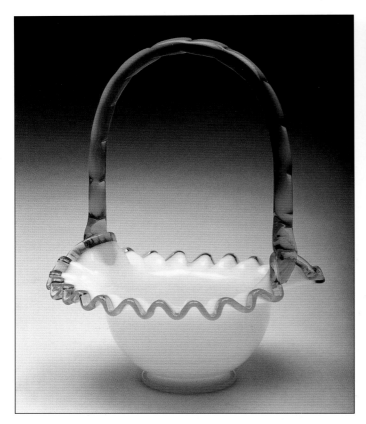

Aqua Crest, #203, 8" tall, 6.5" wide,
General Catalog 1941 to 1943, **$75**

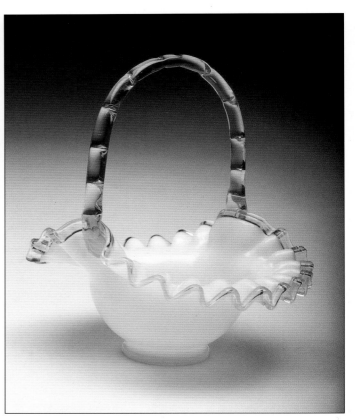

Rose Crest, #203, 7.5" tall, 7.25" wide,
General Catalog 1946 to 1948, **$55**

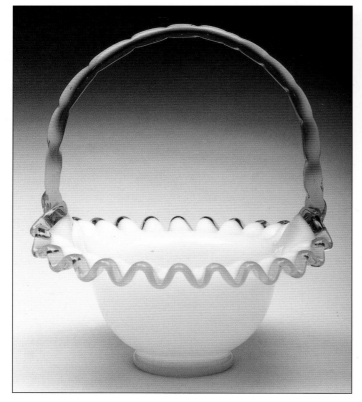

Gold Crest, #203, 7.5" tall, 7" wide,
General Catalog 1943 to 1944, **$45**

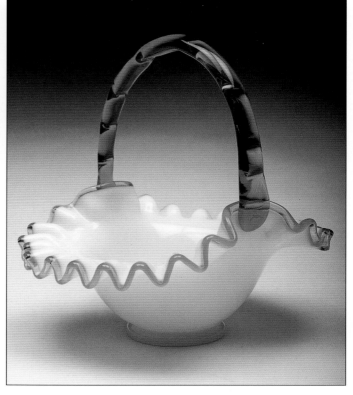

Emerald Crest, #7237EC, 6.75" tall, 7" wide,
General Catalog 1952 to 1955, **$98**

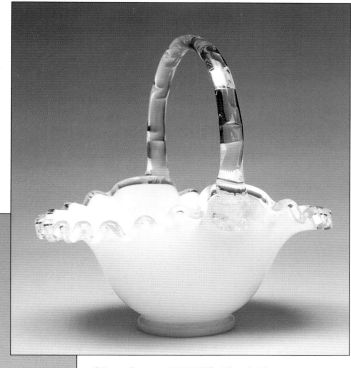

Silver Crest, #7237SC, 7" tall 6" wide, crystal handle, General Catalog 1943-1987, **$25**

Silver Crest, #7237SC, 7" tall 6" wide, milk glass handle, General Catalog 1943-1948, **$45**

Black Rose, #7237BR, 8.25" tall, 6.5" wide, General Catalog 1953 to 1954, **$195**

Silver Crest, #7237BY, 8" tall, 6.5" wide, Butterflies on Milk Glass decoration, General Catalog 1977 to 1979, **$38**

Black Snowcrest, #6587, Black with white crest, 6.75" tall, 4.5" wide, Fenton Gift Shop, 2001, **$49**

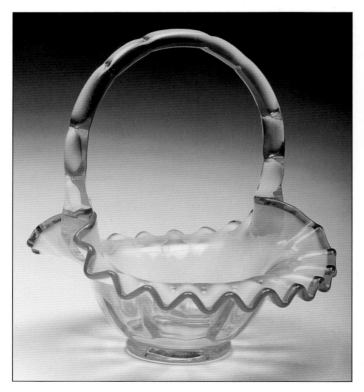

Cobalt Crest, #V5939AK, Blue Topaz Opalescent, 7.5" tall, 7.25" wide, Interior wide panel, Fenton Gift Shop, 2002, **$65**

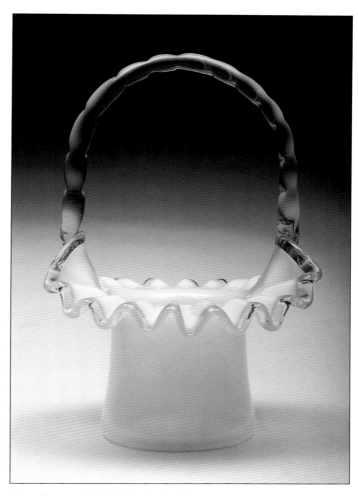

Silver Crest, #36, 6.75" tall 4.75" wide, Charleton
decoration, Abels Wasserburg, 1943 to 1947, **$49**

Rose Crest, #1924, 7" tall, 5" wide,
General Catalog 1946 to 1947, **$60**

Gold Crest, #1924, 7.25"
tall, 5.5" wide, General
Catalog 1943 to 1944, **$45**

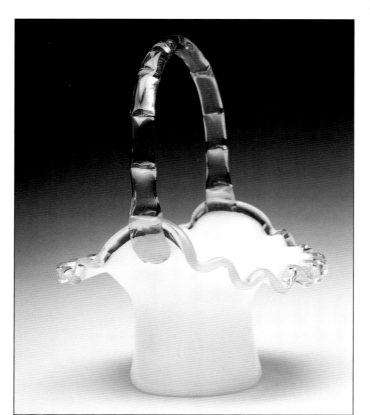

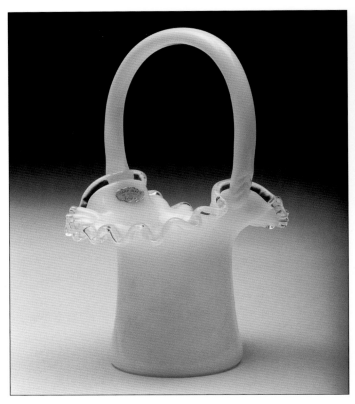

Silver Crest, #1924SC, 6.75" tall, 4.75" wide, General Catalog 1943 to 1952, **$35**

Silver Crest, #1924SC, 6.5" tall, 5" wide, Charleton decoration, milk glass handle, Abels Wasserburg catalog, 1943 to 1952, **$45**

Silver Crest, #1924SC, 6.75" tall, 4.75" wide, Charleton decoration, Abels Wasserburg, 1943-1952, **$48**

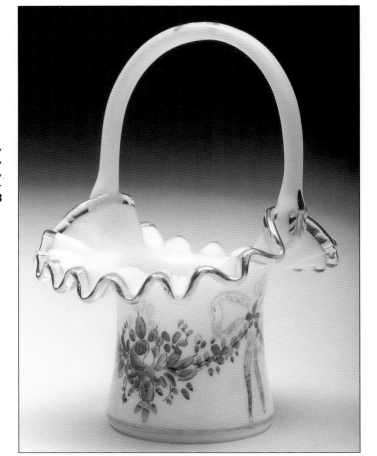

Silver Crest, #7436DV, 6.5" tall 4.75" wide, Violets in the Snow decoration, General Catalog 1968-1980, **$65**

Aqua Crest, #203, 8" tall, 5" wide, General Catalog 1941 to 1942, **$125**

Black Crest, Fenton Gift Shop 1970s, **Left:** #7436BC, 6.5" tall, 4.6" wide, **$125**; **Right:** #7336BC, 6" tall, 8" wide, **$145**

Silver Crest, #7437DV, 7.75" tall, 5" wide, Violets in Snow decoration, 1968 to 1980, **$85**

Black Snowcrest, #7686, Black with Milk Glass crest, 10" tall, 5" wide, Fenton Gift Shop, 2002, **$65**

Plum Crest, #2738PJ, Milk Glass, 7.5" tall, 6.5" wide, Lilacs, decoration designed by Martha Reynolds, Shelley Fenton signature, Family Signature Series, General Catalog, 1994, **$85**

Gold Crest, #203, 7.25" tall, 8" wide,
General Catalog 1943 to 1944, **$98**

Silver Crest, #7234SC, 9.5" tall, 11.5" wide,
General Catalog 1958 to 1980, **$60**

Silver Crest, #7336SC, 7.25" tall, 8" wide,
General Catalog 1957-1986, **$35**

Silver Crest, #7339SC, 8" tall, divided,
General Catalog 1958 to 1960, **$95**

Blue Ridge, #2632BI, French Opalescent with Cobalt crest, 9.75" tall 10.25" wide, June Limited Edition Collectibles Supplement, 80th Anniversary, marked 80th, 1985, **$135**

Ivory Crest, #201, 9.75" tall, 10" wide, General Catalog 1940 to 1942, **$145**

Rose Crest, #192, 10.5" tall, General Catalog 1946 to 1947, **$125**

Blue Ridge, #1920, French Opalescent with Cobalt crest, 13" tall, 12" wide, General Catalog 1938 to 1939, **$375**

Peach Crest, #1523PC, 12.5"
tall, 14" wide, General Catalog
1940 to 1952, **$185**

Silver Turquoise, #7233ST, 13" tall, 1959, **$200**

Peach Crest, #192, 10" tall
10.5" wide, Charleton
decoration on the inside
and gold trim on the
outside, Abels Wasserburg,
1942 to 1948, **$225**

Aqua Crest, #7233AC, 13" tall, General
Catalog 1941 to 1943, **$275**

Silver Crest, #7233SC, 10" tall, 13" wide,
General Catalog 1943 to 1971, **$145**

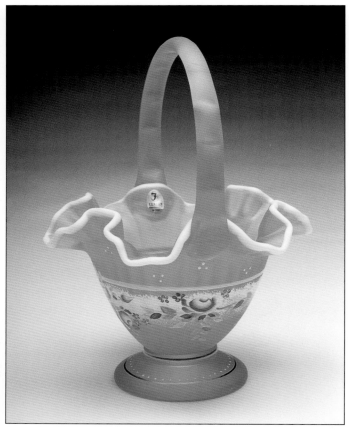

Cloud White Crest, #CV3783F, Blue Topaz satin, 8" tall, 6"
wide, Charleton Collection, Bill Fenton signature, Made for
QVC, January 2002, **$95**
Note: This decoration was inspired by the original Charleton
decoration from the Abels Wasserburg Company.

Sea Mist Green Crest, #CV0371S, Rose Magnolia iridized, 8.75" tall, 8.25" wide, hand painted floral, Bill Fenton signature, Limited to 6000, Made for QVC, August 1993, **$78**

Plum Crest, #CV161JF, 8.5" tall, 8.25" wide, Champayne Iridized, Hand painted with purple flowers, Bill and George Fenton signatures, Inscribed on the bottom: "The ribbon candy edge on this basket is similar to pieces made the first year of production in Williamstown, WV Circa 1907", Made for QVC, March 1997, **$85**

Milk Crest and handle, #CV282TR, Rosalene iridized, 8.75" tall, 8.25" wide, Hand painted with tulips, Bill Fenton signature, Legacy collection, Made for QVC, April 2000, **$110**

Daffodil

A new mould designed by Jon Saffell was patterned after the #7653 footed Daffodil vase. This heavily embossed Daffodil pattern features realistic flowers with leaves radiating up from the base. This basket debuted in the 2004 catalog.

Spruce Green Crest and handle, #CV098AZ, Iridized, hand painted azaleas, Spiral Optic, 90th Anniversary, Made for QVC, June 1995, **$68**

Daffodil, #6532SW, Sunset Stretch, 8.5" tall, 9" wide, Mould designed by Jon Saffell, General Catalog, 2004, **$69**

Autumn Gold Crest, #CV0431B, Iridized milk glass, 10" tall, 7" wide, Hand painted lilies, Bill & Elinor Fenton signatures, Inscribed with the following: Bill & Elinor Fenton Oct. 21, 1943 - Oct. 21, 1993 We share with you in the celebration of our 50 wonderful years together, Made for QVC, December 1993, **$95**

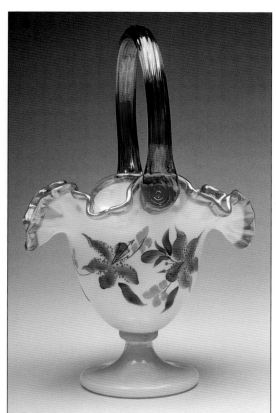

Daisy & Button

This was a pattern that was used by many of the glass companies. George Duncan and Sons were utilizing this pattern as early as 1883. It seemed like each glass house had to have their own version of this pattern.

Frank L. Fenton copied some of the pieces he found in 1936 and 1937. Introduced in 1937, the Daisy & Button pattern was originally called Cape Cod. The new line, #1900, had its name changed a couple of years later to the most familiar name of Daisy & Button. At the L.G. Wright Glass Company of New Martinsville, West Virginia auction, more Daisy & Button moulds were purchased. This was a common pattern and almost every glass company made this pattern.

Daisy & Button, 4" tall, 5.75" wide
Left: #1939CG, Colonial Green, 1963 to 1976, **$22**; **Right**: #1939OR, Orange, 1967 to 1969, **$30**

Daisy & Button, #1939CB, Colonial Blue, 4" tall, 5.75" long, General Catalog, 1969 to 1972, **$35**

Daisy & Button, #1939MI, Milk Glass, 4" tall, 5.75" long, General Catalog 1973 to 1976, **$25**

Daisy & Button, #C1935IP, Iridized Plum Opalescent, 8.25" tall, 6" wide, wings on side, Made for QVC, October 1996, **$45**

Daisy & Button, #1935MI, Milk Glass, 5.5"
tall, 5.5" wide, wings on side, Olde Virginia
Glass catalog, 1973, **$20**

Daisy & Button, #C1935C7, Willow Green Iridized, 5.5" tall 5.5"
wide, wings on side, Black crest, Made for QVC, April 2003, **$38**

Daisy & Button, #22-4, 7.25" tall, 5.25" wide,
Made for LG Wright, 1950s and 1960s
Left: Blue, **$32; Right:** Amber, **$24**

Daisy & Button, #DS507T3, Topaz Opalescent,
7.75" tall, 6" wide, cobalt handle, Made for
Westmoreland Museum Gift Shop, 2002, **$58**

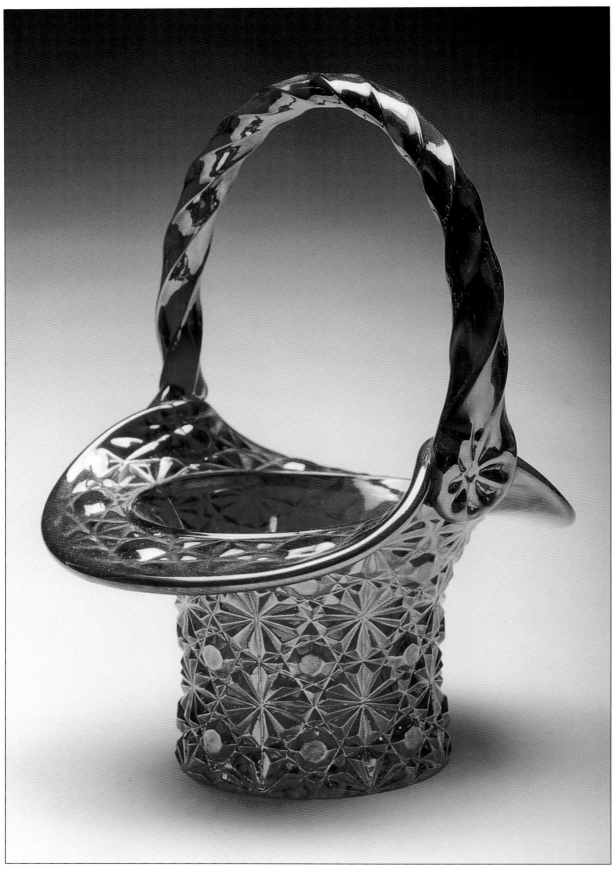

Daisy & Button, #1936RN, Red Carnival, 7.75"
tall, 6" wide, General Catalog 1995, **$48**

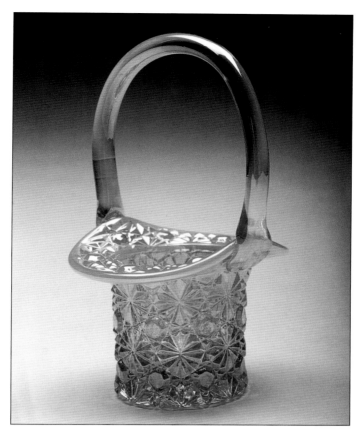

Daisy & Button, #CV021LI, Sea Mist Green Opalescent
Iridized, 5.5 " tall, 3.5" wide, Made for QVC, June 1992, **$35**

Daisy & Button,
#C1936PX, Plum carnival,
8.25" tall, 6" wide, Made
for QVC, June 1995, **$40**

Daisy & Button, #1936SO, Spruce Green, 6" tall, 7" wide, Fenton Gift Shop, 1999, **$42**

Daisy Criss-Cross Optic

Daisy Criss-Cross Optic pattern was a new optic design that was created in 2001. The pattern was inspired by the Beaumont Glass Company pattern of Daisy in Criss-Cross, that dates to the late 19th century. This basket was selected to be part of the Family Signature Series and bears George Fenton's signature.

Right:
Daisy Criss-Cross Optic, #1932CR, Cranberry Opalescent, 7.75" tall, 5.25" wide, Inscribed with George Fenton's signature & numbered on the bottom but was not limited to a set amount (this one in photo is #2573), Family Signature Series General Catalog 2001, **$95**

Daisy & Fern Optic

This pattern was made as early as the late 1890s by Northwood and then later by Dugan Glass. The L.G. Wright mould, purchased from Northwood Glass in Wheeling, West Virginia, was sent to Fenton to make items for the L.G. Wright Glass Company of New Martinsville, West Virginia. Fenton altered the design slightly when they began making this pattern for themselves. The early ones have straight petals on the flowers, while the Fenton ones have a slight curl on each petal.

Daisy & Fern Optic, #1832BX, Sapphire Blue Opalescent, 7.5" tall, 6.5" wide, Collectors Extravaganza Supplement 1990, **$60**

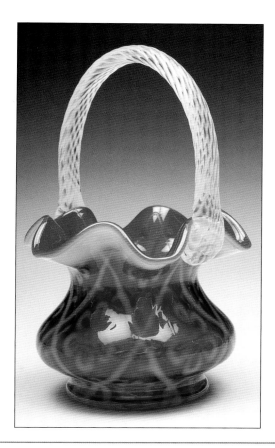

Diamond

This a former mould from the Imperial Glass Company of Bellaire, Ohio. It was called #414 by Imperial but collectors have nicknamed it Diamond Quilted. Imperial made a variety of pieces in the 1920s and 1930s.

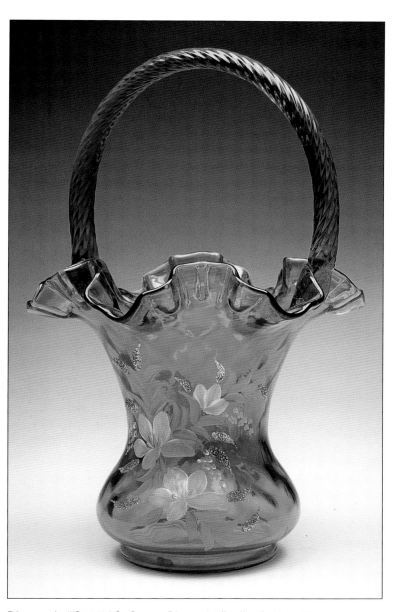

Diamond, #C14458S, Ocean Blue, 10.5" tall, 7" wide, Hand painted floral decoration, Made for QVC, October 1994, **$98**

Daisy Optic

This is a variation of the Daisy & Fern Optic pattern. This special optic is sure to delight collectors. The Daisy Optic is hard to maintain and allow each daisy to look defined.

Daisy Optic, #1739CR, Cranberry Opalescent, 7.5" tall, 6.5" wide, General Catalog 1992, **$125**

Diamond Flute

An original Fenton design that was first used in 1911 on a swung vase. The mould was brought back out when carnival glass was revived in the 1970s.

Diamond Flute, #C29127O, Cobalt Iridized, 8" tall, 7.75" wide, Milk Glass crest, Made for QVC, June 2001, **$45**

Diamond Flute, #2912PY, Champayne, 8" tall, 7.75" wide, General Catalog 1999, **$40**

Diamond Flute, #2917RU, Ruby, 8" tall, 7.75" wide, General Catalog 1985 to 2000, **$48**

Diamond Lace

Etna Glass was located in Bellaire, Ohio and operated from 1880 to 1889. The pattern, Hobnail in Square, by Etna Glass was the inspiration for Frank M. Fenton to design this pattern for use at Fenton. An epergne in Diamond Lace debuted in 1949 at the Pittsburgh gift show for retailers. The epergne was the first piece to be developed. It sold very well and Frank M. Fenton designed several more items.

Diamond Lattice Optic

An early opalescent pattern called Opal Lattice resembles this pattern. Northwood, Dugan, National and Phoenix all made versions of this pattern. The L.G. Wright Glass Company of New Martinsville, West Virginia later produced this pattern for many years.

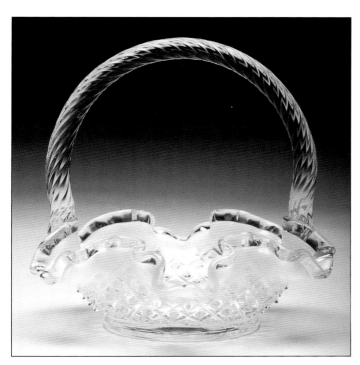

Diamond Lace, #4833YW, French Opalescent, Chiffon Pink crest and handle, 5.5" tall, 6" wide, General Catalog 2001, **$45** **Note:** Chiffon Pink is dichroic glass that turns a different color when photographed. It is actually an intense pink color. This basket pictured in the Fenton catalog has been retouched to create the pink color.

Diamond Lattice Optic, #1131DX, French Opalescent, 8.5" tall, 5.5" wide, Dusty Rose crest, Trellis, decoration designed by Martha Reynolds, Lynn Fenton signature, Family Signature Series, General Catalog, 1995, **$98**

Diamond Lattice Optic, #4830DX, French Opalescent, 8.25" tall, 6" wide, Empress Rose crest and handle, Trellis decoration, decoration designed by Martha Reynolds, Tom Fenton signature, Family Signature Series, General Catalog 1998, **$95**
Note: Empress Rose is a dichroic glass that turns a somewhat different color when photographed. It is actually a pink color.

Diamond Optic, #1502, Ruby, 1.75" tall, 8" wide, metal handle, General Catalog early 1930s, **$45**

Diamond Optic, #1502, Aquamarine, 2.5" tall, 5.75" wide, metal handle, bon bon crimped, General Catalog 1927 to 1931, **$45**

Diamond Optic

Initially, made by many early companies like Buckeye, Beaumont, and Northwood in opalescent colors. The optic mould could be used on any shape. In the early years, Fenton produced this pattern in many transparent colors. For a complete listing of this pattern, please refer to our book, *Elegant Glass: Early, Depression and Beyond.*

Diamond Optic, #1615, Green, 5.75" tall, 9" wide, metal
handle, General Catalog early 1930s, **$60**

Diamond Optic, #1615, Black, 5.75" tall, 9" wide,
metal handle, General Catalog 1927 to 1931, **$85**

Diamond Optic, #1615, Ruby, 5.75" tall, 10.5" wide,
metal handle, General Catalog mid 1930s, **$125**

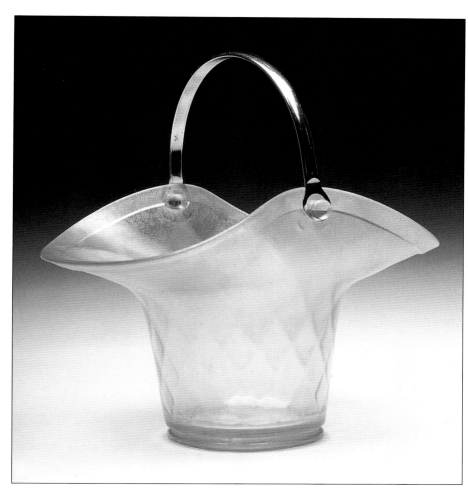

Diamond Optic, #1615, Aquamarine stretch, 5.75" tall, 8.75" wide, metal handle, General Catalog 1927 to 1931, **$175**

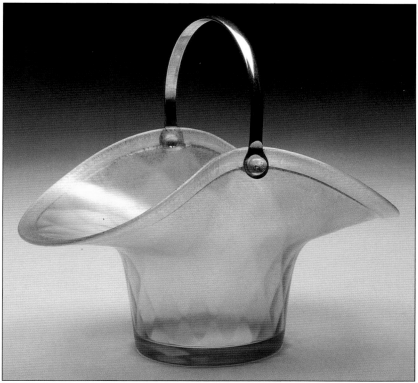

Diamond Optic, #1615, Velva Rose, 5.5" tall, 9.75" wide, 9", metal handle, General Catalog 1926-28, **$125**

Diamond Optic, #1924, Mulberry, 6.75" tall, 4.75" wide, General Catalog 1942, **$125**

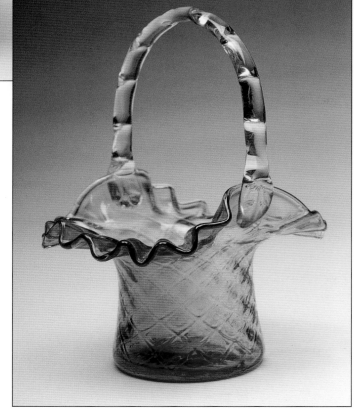

Diamond Optic, #1924, Ruby Overlay, 6.75" tall, 4.75" wide, General Catalog 1942 to 1948, **$68**

Diamond Optic, #1924, Ruby Overlay, 7" tall,
6" wide, General Catalog 1942 to 1948, **$78**

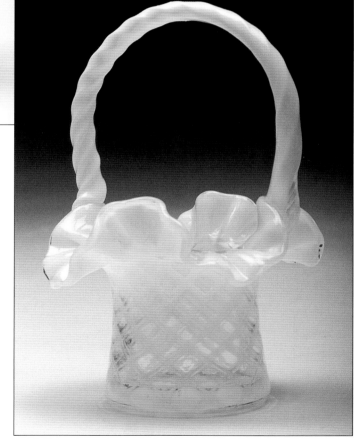

Diamond Optic, #1532TO, 6.75" tall, 4.5" wide,
Topaz Opalescent with milk handle, Fenton Art
Glass Collectors of America (FAGCA) convention
special glass room, 1997, **$85**

Diamond Optic, 5" tall, Made for QVC
Top Right: #CV172H2, Topaz Opalescent Iridized, Hand painted pink and white floral, August 1997, **$70; Top Left:** #C2186, Blue Topaz Overlay, Hand painted white and violet floral, Made for web site only, February 2003, **$65; Bottom Right:** #CV3861E, French Opalescent, Hand painted purple Hibiscus, Violet crest and handle, May 2002, **$60**

Diamond Optic, #203, Ruby Overlay, 6.75" tall, 7.5" wide, General Catalog 1942 to 1948, **$75**

Diamond Optic, #192, Mulberry, 9.25" tall, 10.5" wide, General Catalog 1942, **$400**

Diamond Optic, #1738GO, Green Opalescent, 6.25" tall, 4" wide, General Catalog 1985, **$85**

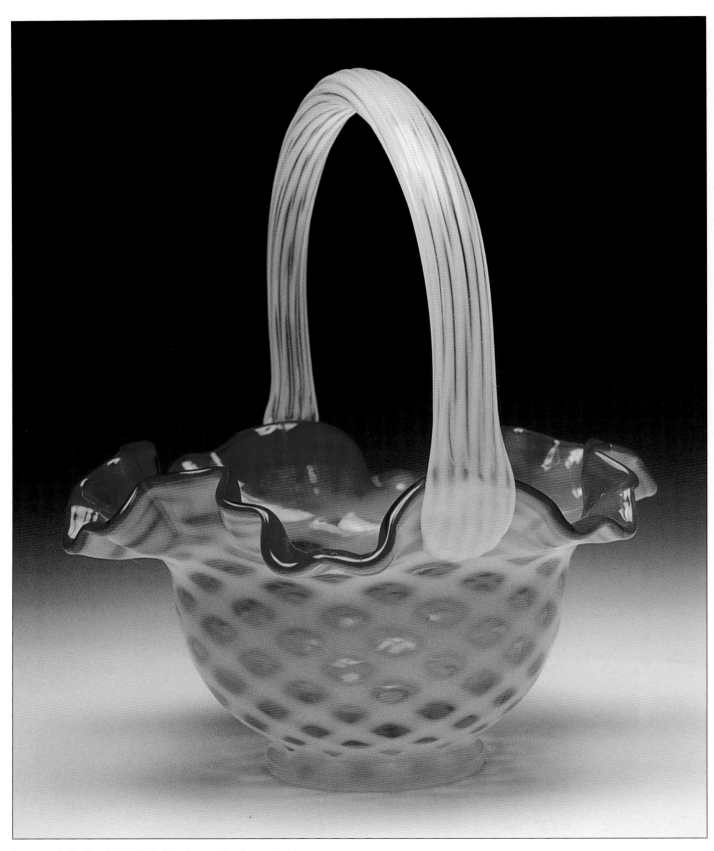

Diamond Optic, #1739CR, Cranberry Opalescent, 7"
tall, 7.5" wide, General Catalog 1990 to 1993, **$75**

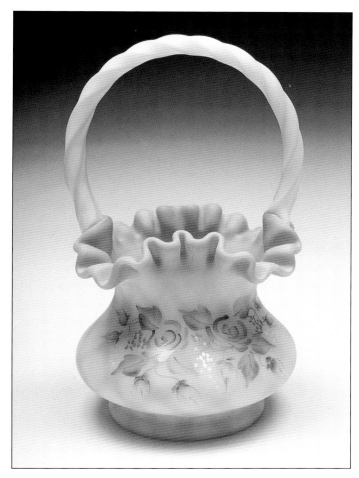

Diamond Optic, #CV204RB, Burmese, 7.75" tall, 4.75" wide, Hand painted with roses, decoration designed by Kim Plauche, Don Fenton signature, Made for QVC, January 1998, **$125**

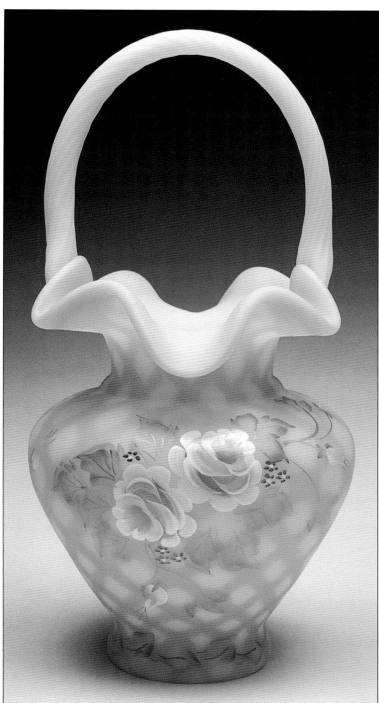

Diamond Optic, #1737CB, Colonial Blue, 9.5" tall 6.25" wide, Experimental treatment, 1962, **No value established**

Diamond Optic, #V51468, Burmese, 10" tall, 5" wide, Heirloom Optics Collection, Frank and George signatures, Decoration designed by Frances Burton, Made for QVC, April 2003, **$89**

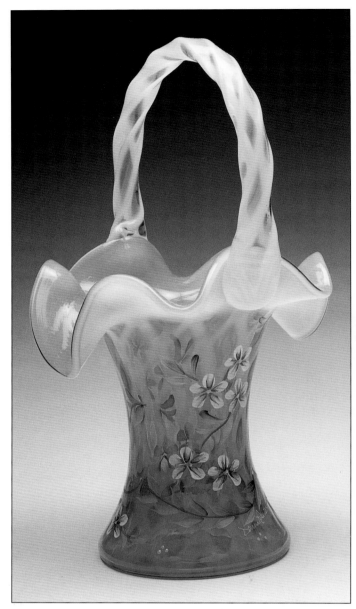

Diamond Optic, #CV259KG, Cobalt Blue Opalescent, 9.5" tall, 6" wide, Hand painted floral decoration designed by Martha Reynolds, Bill Fenton signature, New Century collection, Made for QVC, March 1999, **$99**

Diamond Optic, #CV259N2, Rosemilk, 9.5" tall, 6" wide, Made for QVC, 2003, **$70**
Note: Rosemilk is a dichroic color and turns a different color when photographed. It is actually an intense pink color.

Diamond Optic, #5936, Green 7.5" tall 7.25" wide, Hand painted Poinsettia, Made for Lenox, Scott Fenton signature, **$85**

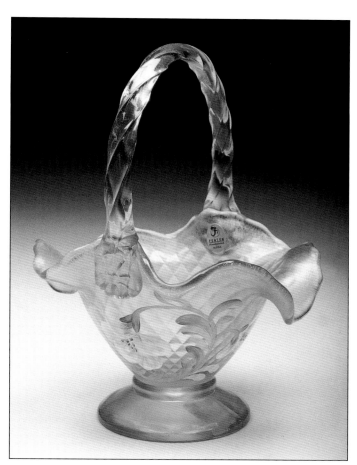

Diamond Optic, #7379S6, Sunset Stretch, 8.5" tall, 6.75" wide, Baroque Floral, decoration designed by Frances Burton, June Supplement 2002, **$75**

Diamond Optic, #1135, 9" tall, 6.5" wide, Blue Opalescent with cobalt handle, Fenton Gift Shop, 1997, **$65**

Diamond Paneled

Diamond Point Columns was developed by Fenton in 1911. This pattern appears to be a variation of that initial pattern.

Diamond Optic, #1135JE, 9.5" tall, 7.25" wide, Celeste Blue with Coralene Floral, decoration designed by Martha Reynolds, 90th anniversary, Bill and Frank Fenton signatures, Family Signature Series, General Catalog 1995, **$85**

Diamond Panel, #1535PX, Amethyst Carnival, 9" tall 5.25" wide, General Catalog 1997, **$50**

Diamond Optic, Made for QVC **Back Left:** #CV53725, Violet Stretch, 9.5" tall, Hand painted Morning Glories, August 2003, **$75; Front Right:** #C86376W, Plum Carnival, 7.5" tall, Hand painted white and pink floral with iced gold lattice, June 1995, **$60**

Dot Optic

Another optic pattern developed from Coin Dot. In the early 1910s several glass companies were making Coin Dot. Dot Optic spot mould gives a good use of contrasting colors in opalescent glass.

Drapery

Northwood Glass in Wheeling, West Virginia made an early opalescent pressed pattern called Drapery. Fenton's pattern resembles this early design and may have been inspired by it.

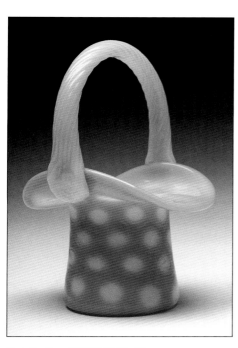

Dot Optic, #DS288UB, Blue Burmese, 6" tall, 4.5" wide, Fenton Gift Shop, 1999, **$75**

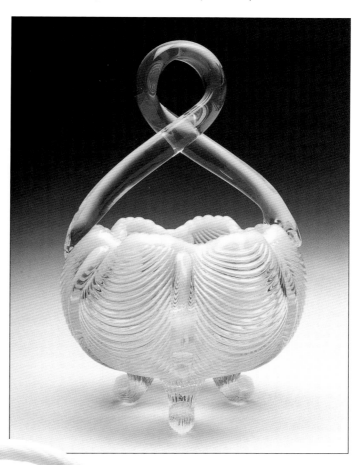

Drapery, #9436TO, Topaz Opalescent, loop handle, 8.25" tall, 5" wide, Limited issue, Collectors Extravaganza Supplement 1988, **$125**

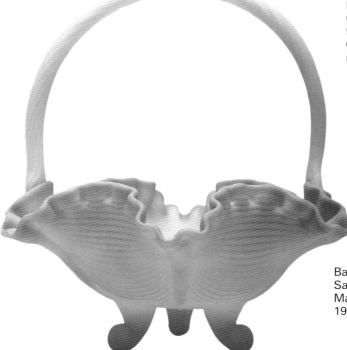

Basket, #C9435R7, Rosalene Satin, 8.25" tall, 8" wide, Made for QVC, November 1992, **$58**

Drapery, #9435RE, Rosalene, 8.5" tall, 8.5" wide, Fenton Gift Shop, 1993, **$68**

Drapery, #CV212AJ, Champayne with Aquamarine crest and handle, 8.5" tall, 8.5" wide, Bill Fenton signature, Made for QVC, Diamond Jubilee collection, March 1998, **$65**

Drapery, #9435XV, Persian Pearl Iridized, 8" tall, 8.5" wide, General Catalog 1993, **$48**

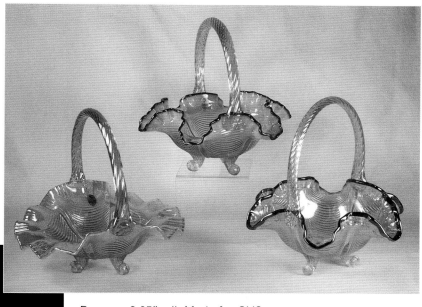

Drapery, 8.25" tall, Made for QVC
Top: #CV212C7, Willow Green Opalescent Iridized, Black crest, October 2002, **$70**
Bottom Left: CV212, Champagne with Willow Green crest and handle, **$65**; **Bottom Right:** #CV2122P, Pink Chiffon Opalescent Iridized, Black Crest, January 2002, **$70**

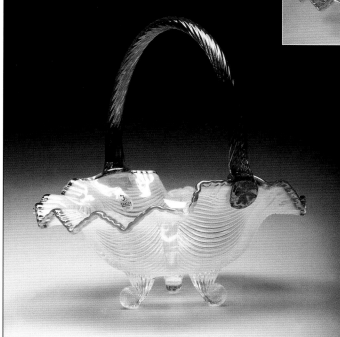

Drapery, #5739YV, French Opalescent Iridized, 8.75" tall, 8.5" wide, Violet crest and handle, Spring supplement 2004, **$65**

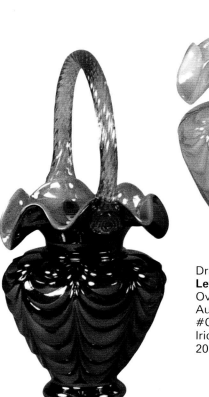

Drapery, Made for QVC
Left: #C3245AG, Amethyst Overlay Iridized, 10.5" tall, August 2002, **$65**; **Right:** #C32451F, Sunset Overlay Iridized, 10.5" tall, August 2002, **$70**

Drapery Optic

The National Glass Company operating at the Northwood Glass Works facility in Pennsylvania advertised an Opal Drapery pattern in 1903. The L.G. Wright Glass Company of New Martinsville, West Virginia later obtained this mould and made several items. The Fenton pattern is of similar design.

Drapery Optic, #2031EH, Fuchsia, 8" tall, 5" wide, General Catalog 1994, **$85**

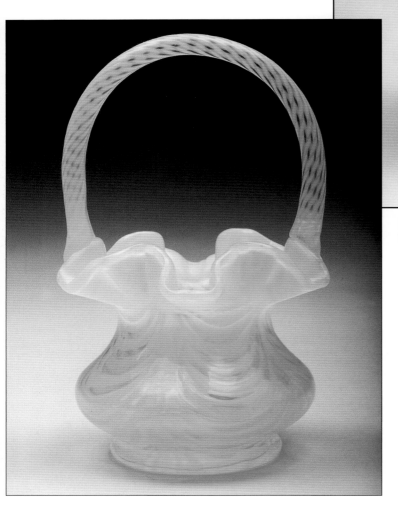

Drapery Optic, #CV428OR, Topaz Opalescent Satin, made for QVC, August 2002, **$90**

Empress

Frank M. Fenton related that he purchased a pressed glass goblet with a feather design. He never did find the name of the pattern. The mould shop made a new mould based on this pattern. Besides the basket, a compote also was made.

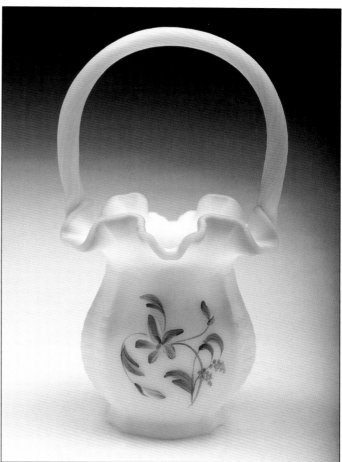

Empress, #4647, Rosalene, satin finish hand painted with wild flowers, 7.25" tall 3.75" wide, Fenton Gift Shop 1991, **$68**

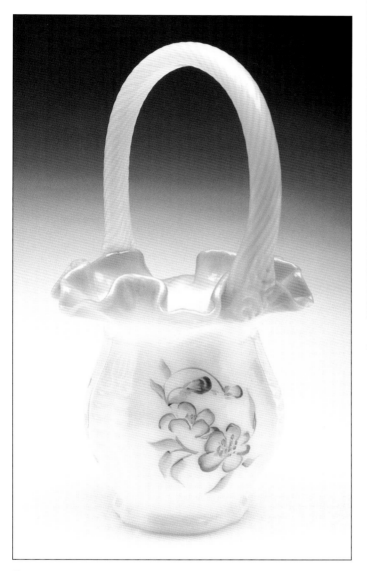

Empress, #4647MD, Rosalene, hand painted with violets, 7.25" tall 3.75" wide, Connoisseur Line 1991, **$68**

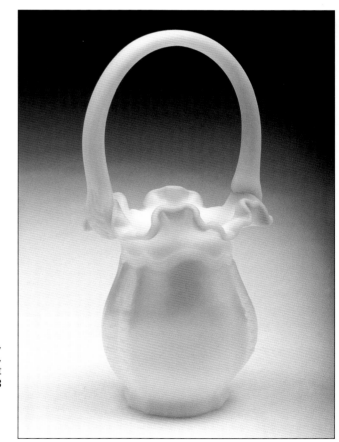

Empress, #4647RE, Rosalene satin, 7.6" tall, 3.75" wide, Fenton Gift Shop, 1992, **$48**

Fabergé

This pattern was designed by Tony Rosena and was inspired by a Fabergé egg. Fenton decided to name the new pattern Fabergé.

Faberge, #CV264CV, Empress Rose Iridized, 5" tall, 4" wide, Made for QVC, June 1999, **$38**
Note: Empress Rose is a dichroic glass that turns a somewhat different color when photographed. It is actually pink.

Faberge, #9431VE, Crystal Velvet, 5.5" tall, 4" wide, General Catalog 1981 to 1982, **$35**

Faberge, #6630EO, Minted Cream, 8.5" tall 7.5" wide, Fenton Gift Shop 1986 to 1988, **$40**

Farmyard

An old carnival pattern originally was made by the Dugan Glass Company of Indiana, Pennsylvania. Singleton Bailey has purchased this mould and had Fenton make him limited edition pieces as part of a special order.

Farmyard, #8833RN, Red Carnival, Jeweled Heart exterior, 8.5" tall, 8.5" wide, Made for Singleton Bailey, 1990s, **$175**

Fern Optic

The idea for this pattern originated with a piece from the Northwood Glass in Wheeling, West Virginia. It features a stylized fern design.

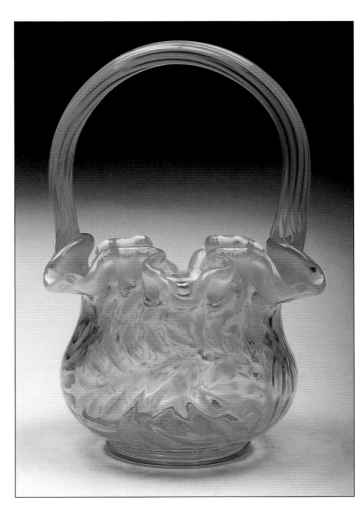

Fern Optic, #1830XC, Persian Blue, 6" tall, 4.25" wide, Collectors Extravaganza 1988, **$45**

Fine Cut & Block

United States Glass Company originally made this pattern in 1891. In the 1950s, Frank M. Fenton saw several pieces in this pattern and purchased them. They were taken back to the mould shop and a new mould was made.

Fine Cut & Block, 7.5" tall, 7" wide, Olde Virginia Glass, 1973 **Left:** #9137CG, Colonial Green, **$24**; **Right:** #9137CA, Amber, **$24**

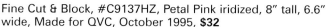

Fine Cut & Block, #C9137HZ, Petal Pink iridized, 8" tall, 6.6" wide, Made for QVC, October 1995, **$32**

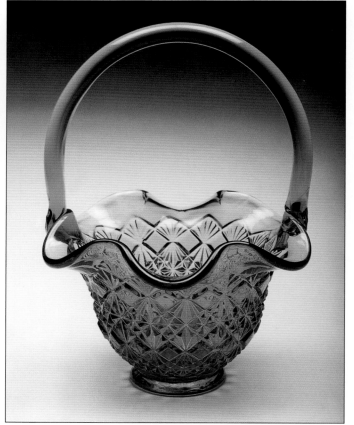

Fine Cut & Block, #9137SO, Spruce Green, 8.25" tall, 6.25" wide, Made for True Value Hardware, 1999, **$30**

Fine Ribbed

This was developed at Fenton. It was utilized during the early carnival period. A series of fine ribs make up the pattern. A sculpted plunger with fine ribs can also be used to make the pattern on the inside of the basket.

Fine Ribbed, #5439IU, Milk Glass, 8" tall, 7.25" wide, Country Pennsylvania, decoration designed by Stacy Williams, Cobalt crest and handle, General Catalog 2004, **$85**

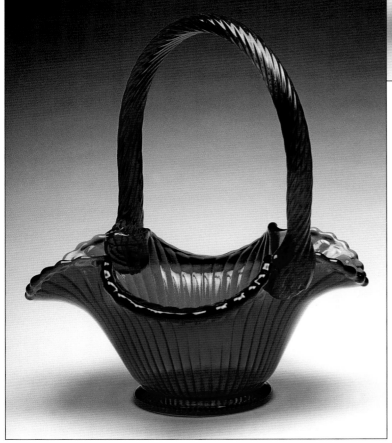

Fine Ribbed, #2787KN, Cobalt, 7.5" tall, 7.25" wide, General Catalog 1995, **$28**

Fine Ribbed, #2787FE, French Opalescent, 7.5" tall, 7.25" wide, Woodland Frost, decoration by Robin Spindler, Christmas Supplement 1999 to 2000, **$48**

Fine Ribbed, #I2787HP, Iridized satin French Opalescent, 7.5" tall, 6.5" wide, Hand painted hummingbird and morning glory, Made for QVC.com, 1999, **$45**

Fine Ribbed, #2787CD, Empress Satin, 7.5" tall, 7.25" wide, Daisies, decoration designed by Kim Plauche, General Catalog 2001, **$65**

Fine Ribbed, #5430KE, Cobalt, 8" tall, 6" wide, Jolly Snowman, decoration designed by Martha Reynolds, Christmas Supplement 2000, **$65**

Fine Ribbed, #6833FE, French Opalescent Iridized, 8.5" tall, 6.75" wide, Woodland Frost, decoration designed by Robin Spindler, Emerald Green crest and handle, Christmas Supplement 2001, **$65**

Fine Ribbed, #68331L, Black, 8.5" tall, 6.75" wide, Midnight Safari, General Catalog 2002, **$85**

Fine Ribbed, #6833HU, Ruby, 8.5" tall 6.75" wide, Winter Seasons, General Catalog 2002, **$75**

Fine Ribbed, #5430U8, Ruby Amberina Stretch, 8" tall, 6" wide, Wine Country, decoration designed by Frances Burton, Don Fenton signature, Family Signature series, limited to sales from January 1 to May 15, General Catalog 2003, **$85**

Fine Ribbed, Made for QVC
Left: #I2787HP, French Opalescent, 8.5" tall, 6.75" wide, Hand painted with floral, Gold Crest, Sold only on web site, May 2001, **$60 Center**: #C68331C, Ice Blue, 8.5" tall, 6.75" wide, Hand painted with pansies, Violet crest, June 2001, **$70; Right**: #CV511MG, Rosemilk Opalescent, 8.5" tall, 6" wide, Hand painted poppies, April 2003, **$60**
Note: Rosemilk is a dichroic glass that turns a different color when photographed. It is actually an intense pink color. When this basket appeared in the Fenton catalog, the photograph was retouched to create the pink color.

Fine Ribbed, #5430 Celeste Blue Stretch, 8" tall 7.25" wide, General Catalog 2004
Left: #5430KP, Dancing Daisies, decoration designed by Stacy Williams, **$75**; **Right**: 5430KA, **$50**

Fine Ribbed, #3097ZB, Black, 10" tall, 6.5" wide, Pumpkin with Cobwebs, Halloween Supplement, 2004, **$85**

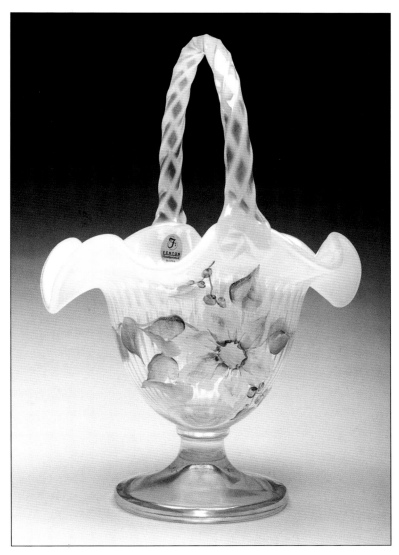

Fine Ribbed, #3097FJ, French Opalescent Iridized, 9.5" tall, 6.75" wide, Royal Lenton Rose, decoration designed by Kim Barley, Christmas Supplement 2003, **$78**

Fine Ribbed, #3097QB, Black, 10" tall, 7" wide, Blue Hydrangeas on Black, decoration designed by Kim Barley, General Catalog 2004, **$90**

Fine Ribbed, Made for QVC
Front Left: #C3097I9, Sunset Stretch, 10" tall, Hand painted vining floral in corals, August 2004, **$85;**
Back Right: #CV283BU, Spruce Green Opalescent, 10" tall, Hand painted with white and purple Peruvian lilies, decoration designed by Martha Reynolds, Violet crest and handle, New Century Collection, 12 Fenton family signatures, November 1999, **$98**

Floral Diamond

McKee Glass of Jeannette, Pennsylvania had a full line of items called Prescut to imitate cut glass. The pattern came from this line.

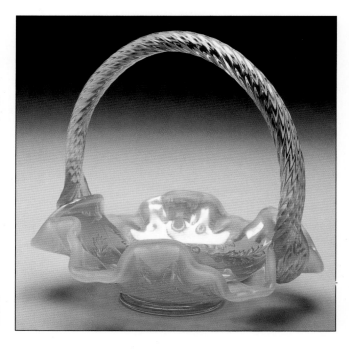

Floral Diamond, #6588G1, Willow Green Opalescent, 6" tall, 6" wide, Historic Collection, General Catalog 2001, **$35**

Georgian

This is an original Fenton design. Many other glass companies such as Cambridge, Duncan, Hocking, New Martinsville, Paden City, and Viking had their own versions of Georgian.

Georgian, #7644, 1980s, Made for Fenton Gift Shop
Left: Mandarin, 6.5" tall, 4.5" wide, **$60**; **Center:** Mandarin Iridized,
6" tall, 4" wide, **$70**; **Right:** Red Carnival, 6" tall, 5.25" wide, **$70**

Georgian, Made for QVC
Left: #CV52536, Rosemilk Opalescent, Hand painted crocuses, Violet crest, May 2003, **$58**; **Right:** #CV1166V, Plum Stretch, Hand painted with floral, Frank M. Fenton signature, October 1995, **$50**
Note: Rosemilk is a dichroic glass that turns a different color when photographed. It is actually an intense pink color. When this basket appeared in the Fenton catalog, the photograph was retouched to create the pink color.

Georgian, #CV117LC, Ice Blue, 4.5" tall,
3.5" wide, Fenton Gift Shop, 1999, **$30**

Grape & Cable, #CV131IP, Iridized Plum Opalescent, 10" tall,
12" wide, Made for QVC, December 1996, **$110**

Grape & Cable

The Grape & Cable pattern featured embossed grapes that are hung on a vine like cable. Harry Northwood developed this pattern for his company. Many different early carnival glass pieces were made. Fenton developed a very close variation of this pattern.

Grape & Cable,
#9074RN, Red
Carnival, 10" tall, 10"
wide, General
Catalog 1990, **$100**

Hanging Heart

The Hanging Heart pattern originated at Fenton in the early 1920s. It was used on freehand glassware. Robert Barber came to work for Fenton in 1974 after operating his own glass operation for a number of years. At Fenton he was given free rein to develop new freehand ware and it was suggested he use the earlier hanging heart design. The Barber collection debuted in 1975 and featured several Hanging Heart pieces along with other unique designs.

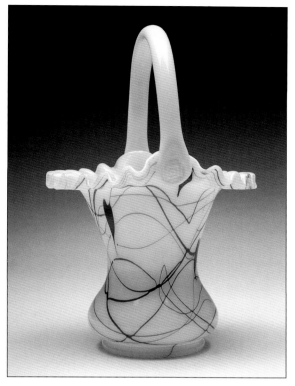

Hanging Heart, #8939CI, Custard, 10.4" tall, 6.5" wide, General Catalog 1976, **$225**

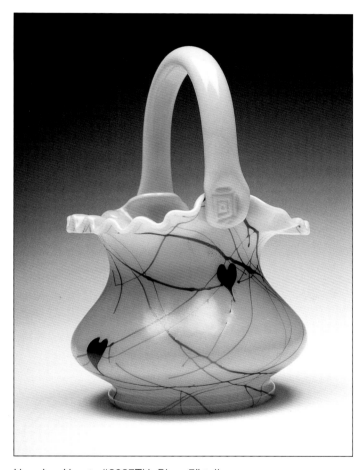

Hanging Heart, #8937TH, Blue, 7" tall, 4.75" wide, General Catalog 1976, **$185**

Heart of America

There are several carnival glass clubs in the United States. They have Fenton make special items for them. Two of these organizations are Heart of America Carnival Glass Association and the America Carnival Glass Association. Both have special pieces pictured here.

Left: Seacoast, Red Carnival, bottom reads: Canandaigua, NY, Made for American Carnival Glass Association (ACGA), 1984, **$60; Center**: Butterfly & Berry, Interior reads: Good Luck HOAGA, Red Carnival, 1984, **$75; Right**: Twilight Blue footed, Sample, 1990s, **No value established**

Heart Optic

Fenton developed the Heart Optic optic for use by the DeVilbiss Perfume Company in the 1940s and 1950s. This special optic was brought back in 1992 to the delight of many collectors. The Heart Optic is hard to maintain and allow the design to look like hearts.

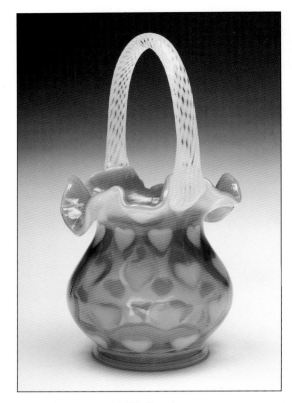

Heart Optic, #2736CR, Cranberry Opalescent, 6.5" tall, 4" wide, Sentiments Collection 1994, **$85**

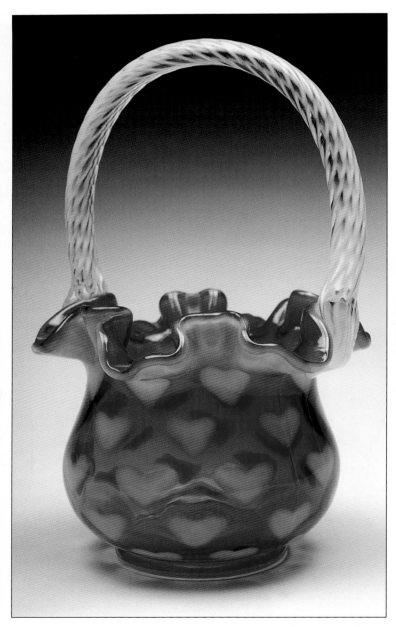

Heart Optic, #6567CR, Cranberry Opalescent, 6.5" tall, 4" wide, Spring Supplement 1992, **$85**

Heart Optic, #6567CR, Cranberry Opalescent satin, 6.25" tall, 4" wide, Fenton Gift Shop, 1992, **$95**

Heart Optic, #4965CR, Cranberry Opalescent, 6.75" tall, 4.25" wide, Spring Supplement 1997, **$85**

Heart Optic, #1924CR, Cranberry Opalescent, 6.75" tall, 4.75" wide, Made for Fenton Art Glass Collectors of America, 1992, **$85**

Heart Optic, #2732CR, Cranberry Opalescent, Caprice, 7" tall, 4" wide, Spring Supplement 1993, **$85**

Heart Optic, #2176CR, Cranberry Opalescent,
10" tall, 4.75" wide, Limited to 2950, Spring
Supplement 2002, **$125**

Heart Optic, #2176, Cranberry
Opalescent, 10" tall, 4.75" wide,
Hand painted, Fenton Gift Shop
2002, **$175**

Hearts & Flowers

This was an original pattern that was first used at Northwood Glass, in Wheeling, West Virginia. Fenton developed their own mould from a bowl that was purchased. Fenton first utilized this pattern when their carnival glass production was revived in the 1970s.

Hearts & Flowers, Made for QVC
Left: #CV347G7, Willow Green Opalescent Iridized, 10.5" tall, 12" wide, Violet crest and handle, April 2001, **$75**; **Center:** #C54886H, French Opalescent Iridized, 10.5" tall, 11" wide, Plum crest and handle, Bill Fenton signature, March 1993, **$80**; **Right:** #C5488AH, Champagne Iridized, 10.5" tall, 11" wide, Aquamarine crest and handle, March 1999, **$70**

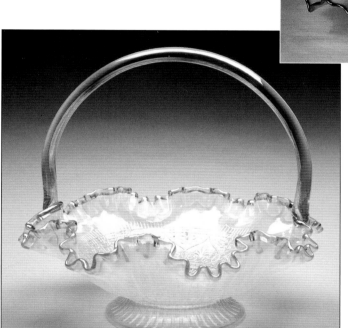

Hearts & Flowers, #C5488IH, Iridized French Opalescent, 10.5" tall, 11" wide, Dusty Rose crest and handle, Made for QVC, March 1992, **$75**

Hexagon

Jon Saffell developed this mould for Fenton in 1996. It features wide panels that form a hexagon shape on the basket.

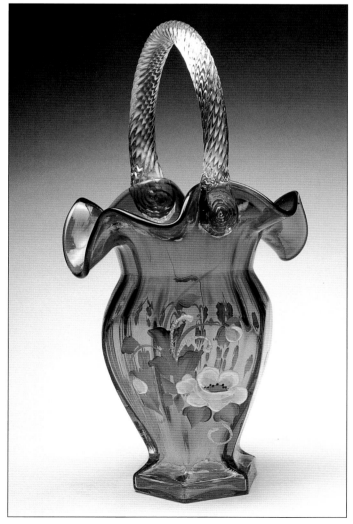

Hexagon, #1533JN, Country Cranberry, 11.25" tall, 6" wide, Roselle on Cranberry decoration, George Fenton signature, Glass Messenger Exclusive, 1996, **$175**

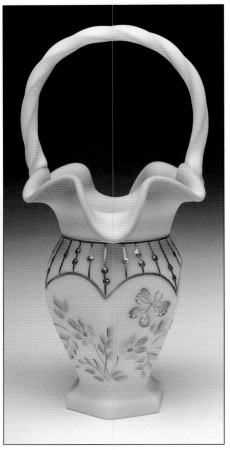

Hexagon, #7632BQ, Burmese, 11.25"
tall, 6" wide, Fenced Garden decoration, Mould designed by Jon Saffell,
Limited to 1750, Connoisseur Collection, 1997, **$175**

Hexagon, #1533, Mulberry, 11.25" tall, 5.75"
wide, floral decoration, Mould designed by
Jon Saffell, Fenton Gift Shop, 1996, **$185**

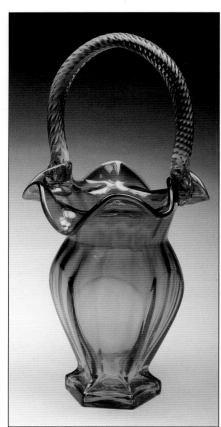

Hexagon, #1533, Gold
Amberina, 11.25" tall,
5.75" wide, Mould
designed by Jon
Saffell, Fenton Gift
Shop, 1999, **$145**

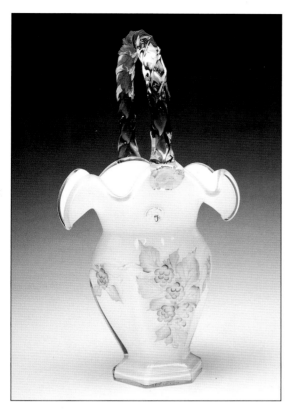

Hexagon, #CV208E8, Opal cased, 11.75" tall, 6" wide, Aquamarine crest, Hand painted with lilacs, Mould designed by Jon Saffell, Bill Fenton signature, Made for QVC Glass Legacy collection, June 2000, **$195**

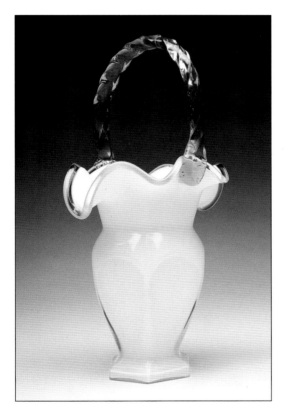

Hexagon, #1533, Milk Glass, 11.75" tall, 6" wide, Aquamarine crest and handle, Mould designed by Jon Saffell, Fenton Gift Shop, 2000, **$125**

Hexagon, 1533EK, Emerald Green, 11.25" tall, 6" wide, Partridge and Pears decoration, Designed by Frances Burton, Mould designed by Jon Saffell, Christmas Supplement, 2002, **$99**

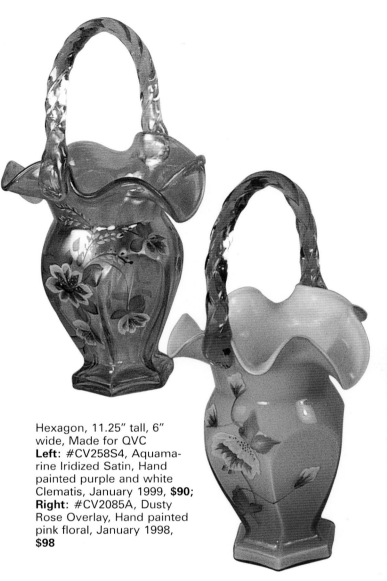

Hexagon, 11.25" tall, 6" wide, Made for QVC
Left: #CV258S4, Aquamarine Iridized Satin, Hand painted purple and white Clematis, January 1999, **$90**;
Right: #CV2085A, Dusty Rose Overlay, Hand painted pink floral, January 1998, **$98**

to have them make a perfume bottle. The piece sold well. Then Fenton made a matching puff box, salt jar, and several other pieces for them. Not wanting to miss out on sales, Fenton decided to make more pieces to sell themselves. The items sold well in the opalescent colors and Fenton continued with Milk Glass. All of these sold extremely well. From there, Fenton made even more Hobnail pieces. Any shape could be used with the hobs being put in the mould. Some ideas for new pieces were inspired by old pieces made by other companies. Since almost every company produced Hobnail, there was a huge assortment to choose from. For a complete listing of this Fenton pattern, please refer to our book, *Elegant Glass: Early, Depression and Beyond*.

The #3634 four-footed and two-handled basket was probably inspired by the Victorian pattern Contessa, which was made by Greener & Company of England.

Hobnail #389 (#3834FO), French Opalescent, 6" tall, 4.75" wide, General Catalog 1940-1956, **$34**

Hobnail

The Hobnail pattern goes back almost to the start of Fenton. Around 1910, swung vases were selling well. Fenton made a Hobnail vase and then swung it out. Today the collectors call this piece Rustic. Next, a Hobnail lamp fount was made for the Lightolier Company in 1935. The takeoff of Hobnail for Fenton resulted from their business with the Wrisley Perfume Company. Wrisley came to Fenton

Hobnail, #389GO, Green Opalescent, 6" tall,
4.75" wide, General Catalog 1940 to 1941, **$90**

Hobnail, #3834CR, Cranberry Opalescent, 6" tall,
4.75" wide, General Catalog 1940 to 1956, **$65**

Hobnail, #389 (#3834TO),
Topaz Opalescent, 6" tall,
4.75" wide, General Catalog
1941-1946 **$68**

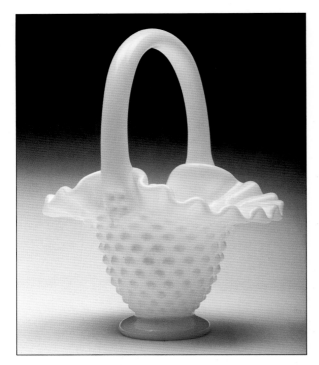

Hobnail, #3834MI, Milk Glass, 6" tall, 4.5" long, General Catalog 1950 to 1989, **$22**

Hobnail, #389, Orchid Opalescent, 6.25" tall, 5" wide, General Catalog mid 1940s, **$85**

Hobnail, #3834BO (389), Blue Opalescent, 6.5" tall, 5" wide, General Catalog 1942 to 1943, **$50**

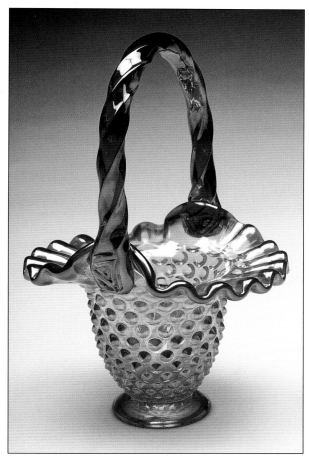

Hobnail, #C3834UG, Sea Mist Green iridized, Cobalt crest and handle, 6.75" tall, 4.5" wide, Made for QVC, August 1995, **$35**

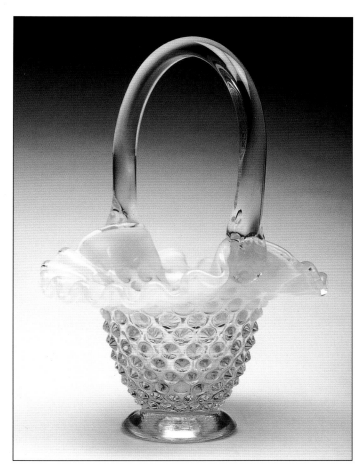

Hobnail, #3834RV, Rose Magnolia, 6.25" tall, 4.5" wide, Historical Collection, 1993, **$45**

Hobnail, #3834UO, 6" tall, 4" wide, Pink Opalescent, Collector's Extravaganza Supplement 1988, **$38**

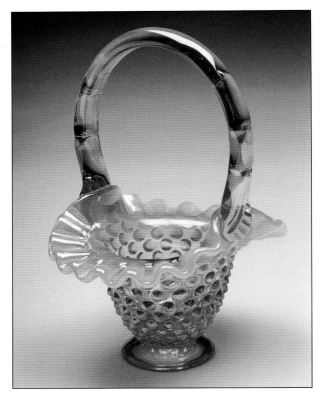

Hobnail, #C3834LK, Misty Blue Iridized, 6.5"
tall, 4.5" wide, Made for QVC, August 1997, **$35**

Hobnail, #K3834GH, French Opalescent with amethyst
handle, 6.25" tall, 4.75" wide, Made for Westmoreland
Museum Gift Shop, 1997, **$38**

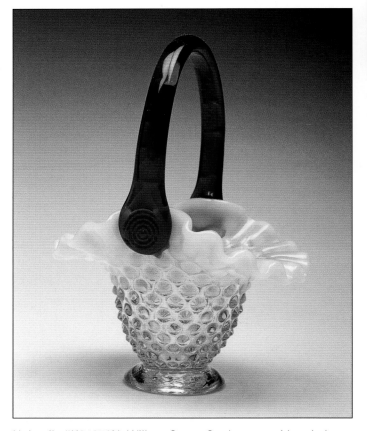

Hobnail, #K84372N, Willow Green Opalescent with cobalt
handle, 6.25" tall 4.75" wide, Made for Westmoreland
Museum Gift Shop, 2001, **$45**

Hobnail, French Opalescent Iridized, 7" tall, 4.5" wide, Spring Supplement 1994 **Left**: #3834FT, Yellow Crest and handle, **$38; Right**: #3834FR, Green Crest and handle, **$38**

Hobnail, #U3834T3, Topaz Opalescent, 6.25" tall, 4.5" wide, Cobalt handle, Made for Westmoreland Museum Gift Shop, 1997, **$49**

Hobnail, Made for QVC
Top: #CV214CR, Cranberry Opalescent, 5" tall, 4.75" wide, Spiral Optic, April 1998, **$65**
Bottom Left: #C3834GY, Willow Green Opalescent Iridized, 5.25" tall, 4.75" wide, April 2000, **$26; Center**: #C3934UG, Sea Mist Green, 6.5" tall, 4.5" wide, Cobalt crest and handle, August 1995, **$40; Right**: #3834LK, Misty Blue Opalescent Iridized, 5.75" tall, 4.75" wide, August 1997, **$26**

Back row left: Hobnail, #389, Topaz Opalescent, 8" tall, 7" wide, General 1943 to 1944, **$145**
Back row right: Hobnail #389 (#3830TO), Topaz Opalescent, 9.5" tall, 10" wide, General Catalog 1959 to 1960, **$175**
Center: Hobnail #389, Topaz Opalescent, 13.5" tall, 10" wide, General Catalog 1941 to 1944, **$500**
Bottom left: Hobnail #389 (#3837TO), Topaz Opalescent, 7.5" tall, 6.75" wide, General Catalog 1959-1961, **$90**
Bottom right: Hobnail #389 (#3834), Topaz Opalescent, 6" tall, 4.75" wide, General Catalog 1941 to 1944, **$68**

Hobnail, #389, Blue, General Catalog 1942 to 1945
Left: 7" tall, 7" wide, **$70**;
Back: 9" tall, 6" wide, **$125**;
Front: 6" tall, 4.5" wide, **$50**;
Right: 11" tall, 10" wide, **$165**

Hobnail, #389, Green, 1940
Left: 6" tall, 4.5" wide, **$65; Center:** 9" tall,
6" wide, **$135; Right:** 10" tall, 10" wide, **$175**

Left: Hobnail,
#6832GY, Willow
Green Opalescent
Iridized, 4.75" tall, 5.5"
wide, General Catalog
2001, **$28**
Right: Hobnail,
#6832OQ, Violet
Iridized, 4.75" tall, 5.5"
wide, General Catalog
2001, **$28**

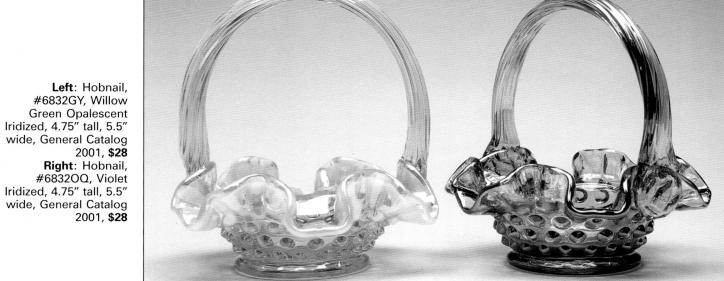

Hobnail, 4.75" tall, 5.5" wide, Made for QVC
Top: #CV229MI, Milk Glass, June 1998, **$24; Bottom Left:** #CV229LK,
Misty Blue Opalescent Iridized, March 1999, **$35: Bottom Right:**
#CV186CR, Cranberry Opalescent, Spiral Optic, October 1997, **$50**

Hobnail, #3634MI, Milk Glass,
4.25" tall, 6" wide, General
Catalog 1963 to 1968; 1979;
1987, **$35**

Hobnail, #C3634IP, Iridized Plum, 4.25" tall, 6" wide, Made for QVC, August 1999, **$49**

Hobnail, #3838MI, Milk Glass, 4.5" tall, 6.5" long,
General Catalog 1960 to 1968, **$24**

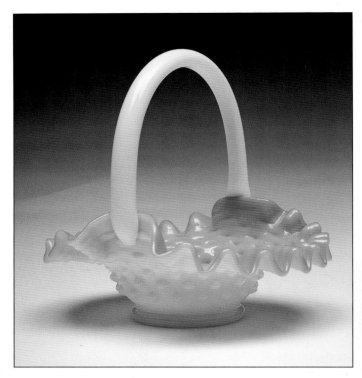

Hobnail, #3835PB, Peach Blow, 5.5" tall, 5.75" wide, General Catalog 1952 to 1956, **$65**

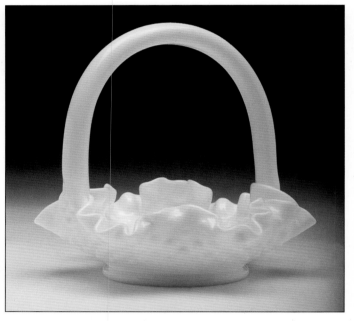

Hobnail, #3735MI, Milk Glass, 5.25" tall, 5.5" wide, General Catalog 1971 to 1984, **$28**

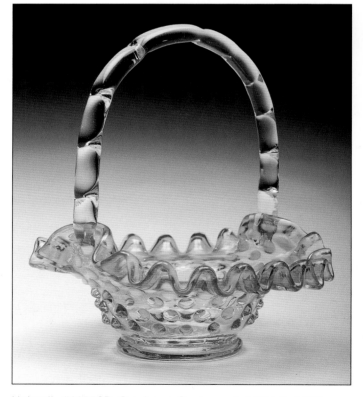

Hobnail, #3835CR, Cranberry Opalescent, 5.5" tall, 5.75" wide, General Catalog 1950 to 1955, **$145**

Hobnail, #1159IM, French Opalescent, 6.5" tall, 5" wide, Green crest and handle, Spring Supplement 1994, **$45**

Hobnail, #3335CR, Cranberry Opalescent, flat hat, 7.5" tall, 8" wide, Fenton Gift Shop, **$75**

Hobnail, #1159IQ, French Opalescent Iridized with cobalt handle, 6.5" tall, 5" wide, Spring Supplement 1995, **$45**

Hobnail, #3335MI, Milk Glass, 7.5" tall, 5.5" wide, loop handle, General Catalog 1970s, **$50**

Hobnail, #3837FO, French Opalescent, 7.5" tall, 7.25" wide, General Catalog 1940 to 1956, **$45**

Hobnail, #A3335UO, Pink Opalescent, 7.5" tall, 5" wide, loop handle, Collectors Extravaganza Supplement 1988, **$58**

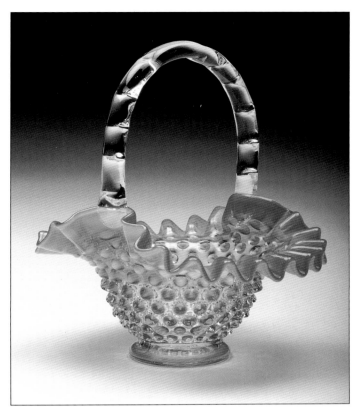

Hobnail, #3837CR, Cranberry Opalescent, 7" tall, 7.25" wide, General Catalog 1941 to 1977, **$98**

Hobnail, #3837RP, Rose Pastel, 7.5" tall, 7" wide, General Catalog 1954 to 1958, **$45**

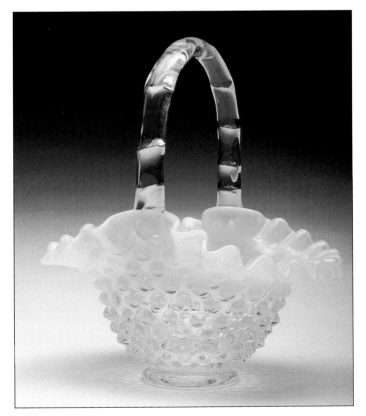

Hobnail, #389 (#3837TO), Topaz Opalescent, 7.5" tall, 7" wide, **$110**

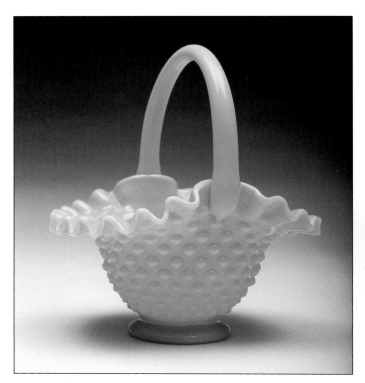

Hobnail, #3837TU, Turquoise, 7.25" tall, 6.75" wide, General Catalog 1955 to 1959, **$65**

Hobnail, #3837CB, Colonial Blue, 7.5" tall, 7" wide, General Catalog 1967 to 1980, **$40**

Hobnail, #3837CA, Colonial Amber, 7.5" tall, 7" wide, General Catalog 1967 to 1971, **$24**

Hobnail, #3837CG,Colonial Green, 7.5" tall, 6.75" wide, General Catalog 1967 to 1977, **$25**

Hobnail, #3837RW, Milk Glass, 7" tall, 6.75" wide, Decorated Hobnail Roses, General Catalog 1974 to 1976, **$40**

Hobnail, #3837OR, Orange, 7.75" tall, 7" wide, General Catalog 1965 to 1977, **$35**

Hobnail, #3837CO, Cameo Opalescent, 7.75" tall, 7" wide, General Catalog, 1979 to 1980, **$49**

Hobnail, #3837MI, Milk Glass, 7.5" tall, 6.75" wide, General Catalog 1950 to 1989 and reissued 1991, **$30**

Hobnail, #3837RU, Ruby, 7.5" tall, 7" wide, General Catalog 1983 to 1986, **$60**

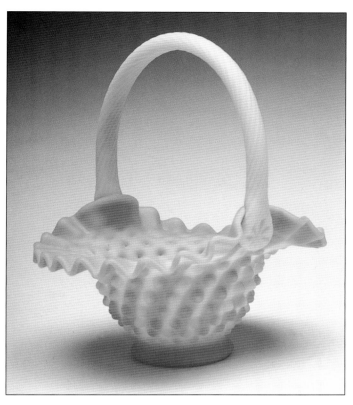

Hobnail, #G5007BR, Burmese, Spiral Optic, 7.75" tall, 7" wide, Fenton Gift Shop February sale, 1996, **$95**

Hobnail, #C3837RZ, Black Rose, 7.5" tall, 7" wide, Frank M. Fenton signature, Made for QVC, August 1992, **$85**

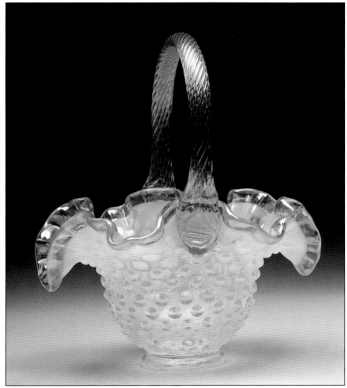

Hobnail, #1158FT, French Opalescent Iridized with Autumn Gold Crest, 7" tall, 6.75" wide, 1994, Spring Supplement 1994, **$45**

Hobnail, #3346CR, Cranberry Opalescent, 8" tall, 7.25" wide, General Catalog 1994 to 2004, **$78**

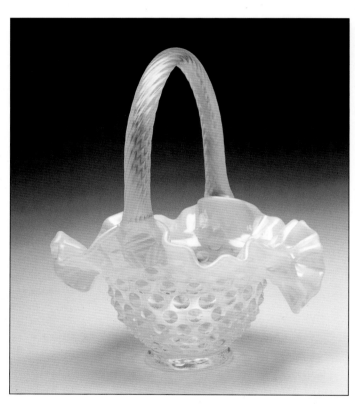

Hobnail, #1158TS, Topaz Opalescent Iridized, 7.5" tall, 7" wide, General Catalog 1997, **$75**

Hobnail, 8" tall, 7.25" wide, Made for QVC
Top: #C3346MI, Milk Glass, December 1996, **$32;**
Bottom: #C1169CR, Cranberry Opalescent, Spiral Optic, October 1993, **$90**

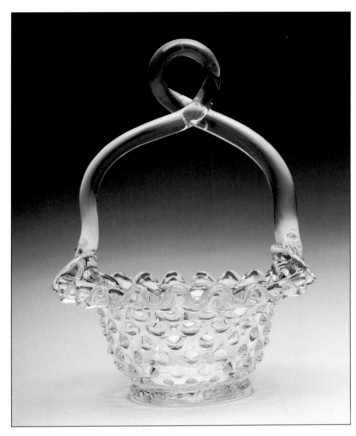

Hobnail, #3837CY, Crystal, 7" tall, 5" wide, loop handle, General Catalog 1968, **$49**

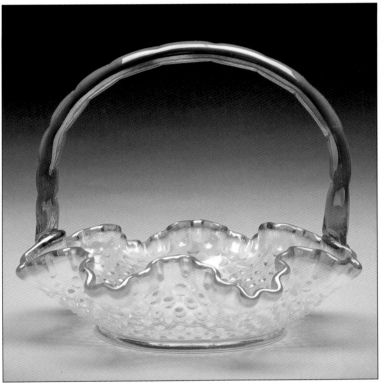

Hobnail, #3736F3, French Opalescent iridized, 6.75" tall, 8" wide, Aqua Crest and handle, Easter Supplement 1993, **$55**

Hobnail, #3736MI, Milk Glass, 6.5" tall, 7.5" wide, General Catalog 1958 to 1984, **$35**

Hobnail, #3638MI, Milk Glass, 7.5" tall, 7.5" wide, roped
panels, General Catalog 1967 to 1989; 1991 to 1992, **$40**

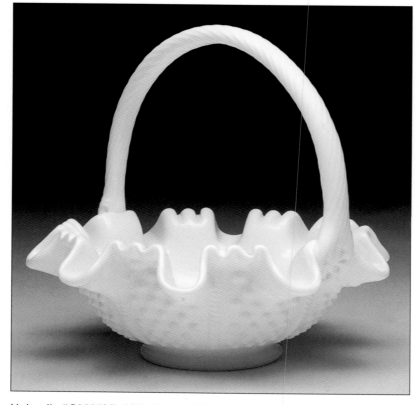

Hobnail, #C3638MI, Milk Glass, 7.5" tall, 7.5" wide,
roped panels, Made for QVC, March 1996, **$48**

Hobnail, #3638CA, Colonial Amber, 7.5" tall, 7.5" wide, roped panels, General Catalog 1967 to 1980, **$32**

Hobnail, #3678M1, French Opalescent Iridized, 8" tall, 9.5" wide, Willow Green crest and handle, Spring Supplement 2003, **$65**

Hobnail, #3678YV, French Opalescent
iridized, 8.25" tall, 9.5" wide, Violet crest and
handle, Spring Supplement 2003, **$65**

Hobnail, #389, Topaz Opalescent, 9.5" tall, 9.75" wide, **$98**

Hobnail, #1156FD, French Opalescent
Iridized, 9.5" tall, 9" wide, Dusty Rose Crest
and handle, Easter Collection, 1993, **$65**

Hobnail, #3638RU, 9" tall, 11" wide, Ruby,
General Catalog 1987 to 1988, **$85**

Hobnail, #389 (#3830TO), Topaz Opalescent, 9.5" tall,
10" wide, General Catalog 1959 to 1960, **$175**

Hobnail, #3830CR, Cranberry Opalescent, 9.5" tall
9.75" wide, General Catalog 1940-1969, **$185**

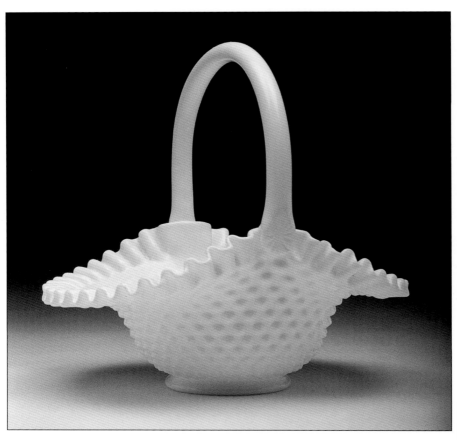

Hobnail, #3830MI, Milk Glass, 9.25" tall, 9.5"
wide, General Catalog 1953 to 1989, **$50**

Hobnail, #3830CB, Colonial
Blue, 9" tall, 9.75" wide, General
Catalog 1968 to 1978, **$48**

Hobnail, #A3830UO, Pink Opalescent, 9.25" tall, 9.75" wide, Collectors Extravaganza 1988, **$100**

Hobnail, #3348CR, Cranberry Opalescent, 9.5" tall, 10.5" wide, General Catalog 1994 to 1996, **$125**

Hobnail, #CV169IH, French Opalescent with Dusty Rose crest, 9.5" tall, 10.25" wide, Made for QVC Museum Collection, March 1997, **$68**

Hobnail, #3734MI, Milk
Glass, 10" tall, 11.5" wide,
General Catalog 1959-1989
and later reissued 1994 to
1995, **$58**

Hobnail, #389, Topaz Opalescent, 9"
tall, 5.75" wide, cone, **$150**

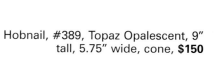

Hobnail, #389, Blue Opalescent, 9" tall, 5.75" wide, cone, **$125**

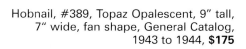

Hobnail, #389, Topaz Opalescent, 9" tall, 7" wide, fan shape, General Catalog, 1943 to 1944, **$175**

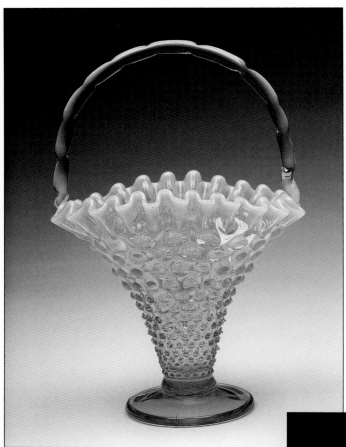

Hobnail, #389, Blue Opalescent, 9" tall, 7" wide, fan shape, General Catalog, 1942 to 1943, **$150**

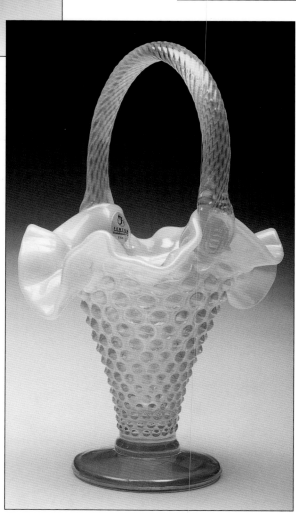

Hobnail, #3637CR, Cranberry Opalescent, 9.75" tall, 6.75" wide, deep, General Catalog 1963 to 1965, **$400**

Hobnail, 3357GY, Willow Green Opalescent, 9" tall, 5.5" wide, General Catalog, 2001, **$48**

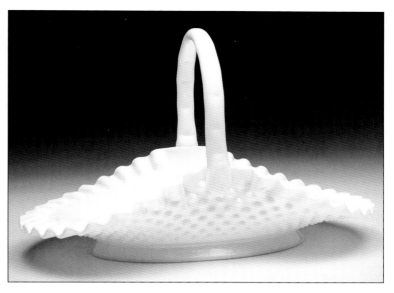

Hobnail, #3839MI, Milk Glass, 8.25" tall, 12.75" long, oval
May style, General Catalog 1960 to 1974, **$78**

Hobnail, #3637MI, Milk Glass, 9" tall, 6.75" wide,
General Catalog 1963 to 1977, **$75**

Hobnail, #3839PO, Plum Opalescent, 9.25" tall, 13" long, oval
May style, General Catalog 1959 to 1962, **$295**

Hobnail #389, Topaz Opalescent, 13.5" tall, 10"
wide, General Catalog 1941 to 1944, **$500**

Holly

An old Fenton carnival glass pattern that dates back to 1911. A simple pattern of sprigs of holly radiating from the center of the piece seems to work quite well.

Holly, 8" tall, Made for QVC
Top: #CV022HU, Petal Pink Satin Iridized, December 1995, **$40**
Bottom Left: #CV022PI, Plum Opalescent Iridized, June 1994, **$55;**
Bottom Right: #CV022RN, Red Carnival, November 1992, **$50**

Hummingbird

Jon Saffell designed a new plunger for the Hummingbird basket. Jon has said, "It was a challenge to sculpt the figure on the plunger, because it had to be carved in reverse. Also, because of the slope of the plunger sides, the figure had to be very shallow to allow the plunger to pull away from the glass without tearing the glass." This design was done in 1997.

Hummingbird, #5731PX, Plum Carnival, 7.25" tall, 8" wide, General Catalog 1997, **$49**

Collector Information

No matter what pattern you collect, we encourage you to belong to a nonprofit organization that works to preserve the history of the American glass making industry. These organizations enable you to gather more information on a particular glass company. All of the national organizations listed below provide information by publishing an educational newsletter, doing study guides, reprinting of company catalogs, doing seminars, holding a convention, having a museum and presenting other educational activities.

Pacific NW Fenton Association
P. O. Box 881, Tillamook, OR 97141
Phone contact: 503-842-4815
23/year   4 newsletters "The Fenton Nor'Wester" and exclusive piece of Fenton glass
Email: jshirley@oregoncoast.com
Web site: www.glasscastle.com/pnwfa.htm
Info: Sponsor two glass shows (March & October) called "All American Glass Show & Sale" in Hillsboro, Oregon and a convention is held in June of each year in Eugene, Oregon

Fenton Art Glass Collectors of America
P. O. Box 384, Williamstown, WV 26187
Phone contact: 304-375-6196
$20/year   6 newsletters "Butterfly Net"
Email: kkenworthy@foth.com
Web site: www.collectoronline.com/club-FAGCA.html
Info: Convention in August

National Fenton Glass Society
P. O. Box 4008, Marietta, OH 45750
Phone contact: 740-374-3345
$35/year   6 newsletters "Fenton Flyer"
Email: nfgs@ee.net
Web site: www.fentonglasssociety.org
Info: Convention in August

Glass Messenger
700 Elizabeth Ave., Williamstown, WV 26187
Phone contact: 1-800-249-4527
$12/year   4 issues and a voucher for the purchase of an exclusive subscriber item

West Virginia Museum of American Glass
P. O. Box 574, Weston, WV 26452
$25/year   4 newsletters "All About Glass" formerly Glory Hole
Email: tbredehoft@nextek.net
Web site: http//members.aol.com/wvmuseumofglass
Info: Convention in October

Web Sites

Fenton Art Glass Company
www.fentonartglass.com

Fenton Forum: www.forum.fentonartglass.com

Fenton Fanatics: www.fentonfan.com
Courtesy of John Gager, Webmaster

Bibliography

Books

Burns, Carl. The *Collector's Guide to Northwood's Carnival Glass*. Gas City, Indiana: L-W Books, 1994.

Burns, Carl. *Dugan and Diamond Carnival Glass*. Paducah, Kentucky: Collector Books, 1999.

Burns, Carl. *Imperial Carnival Glass*. Paducah, Kentucky: Collector Books, 1996.

Coe, Debbie and Randy. *Fenton Burmese Glass*. Atglen, Pennsylvania: Schiffer Publishing, 2004.

Coe, Debbie and Randy. *Elegant Glass: Early, Depression and Beyond*. Atglen, Pennsylvania: Schiffer Publishing, 2004.

Edwards, Bill and Mike Carwile. *Standard Encyclopedia of Opalescent Glass*. Paducah, Kentucky: Collector Books, 1999.

Edwards, Bill and Mike Carwile. *Standard Encyclopedia of Pressed Glass*. Paducah, Kentucky: Collector Books, 2000.

Fenton Art Glass Collectors of America. *Glass made for Fenton Art Glass Collectors of America From 1978 to 2002*. Marietta, Ohio: Richardson Printing Corp., 2003.

Griffith, Shirley. *Pictorial Review of Fenton's White Hobnail Milk Glass*. Warren, Ohio: Shirley Griffith, 1994.

Heacock, Bill. *Fenton Glass The First Twenty Five Years*. Marietta, Ohio: Richardson Printing Corp, 1978.

Heacock, Bill. *Fenton Glass The Second Twenty Five Years*. Marietta, Ohio: O-Val Advertising Corporation, 1980.

Heacock, Bill. *Fenton Glass The Third Twenty Five Years*. Marietta, Ohio: O-Val Advertising Corporation, 1989.

Heacock, Bill with James Measell and Berry Wiggins. *Harry Northwood, The Early Years 1881-1900*. Marietta, Ohio: Antique Publications, 1991.

Heacock, Bill with James Measell and Berry Wiggins. *Harry Northwood, The Wheeling Years 1901-1925*. Marietta, Ohio: Antique Publications, 1990.

Heacock, Bill and William Gamble. *Encyclopedia of Victorian Colored Pattern Glass Book 9 Cranberry Opalescent from A to Z*. Marietta, Ohio: Antique Publications, 1987.

Lechler, Doris Anderson. *Children's Glass Dishes, China & Furniture*. Paducah, Kentucky: Collector Books, 1991.

Measell, James. *Fenton Glass The 1980s Decade*. Marietta, Ohio: The Glass Press, 1996.

Measell, James. *Fenton Glass The 1990s Decade*. Marietta, Ohio: The Glass Press, 2000.

Measell, James. *Fenton Glass Especially for QVC*. Williamstown, West Virginia: Richardson Printing, 2002.

Metz, Alice Hulett. *Early American Pattern Glass*. Columbus, Ohio: Spencer-Walker Press, 1960.

Metz, Alice Hulett. *Much More Early American Pattern Glass*. Columbus, Ohio: Spencer-Walker Press, 1965.

Miller, Robert W. *Mary Gregory and her Glass*. Des Moines, Iowa: Wallace-Homestead Co., 1972.

Rice, Ferill J.. *Caught in the Butterfly Net*. Williamstown, West Virginia: Fenton Art Glass Collectors of America, 1991.

Stout, Sandra McPhee. *The Complete Book of McKee Glass*. North Kansas City, Missouri: Trojan Press, Inc., 1972.

Thistlewood, Glen and Stephen. *The Art of Carnival Glass*. Atglen, Pennsylvania: Schiffer Publishing, 2004.

Thistlewood, Glen and Stephen. *A Century of Carnival Glass*. Atglen, Pennsylvania: Schiffer Publishing, 2001.

Thistlewood, Glen and Stephen. *Carnival Glass, The Magic and Mystery*. Atglen, Pennsylvania: Schiffer Publishing, 1998.

Truitt, R & D. *Mary Gregory Glassware*. Rockville, Maryland: Beach Brothers Printing, 1992.

Walk, John. *Fenton Glass A to Z*. Atglen, Pennsylvania: Schiffer Publishing, 2004.

Walk, John. *Big Book of Fenton Glass 1940 to 1970*, Atglen, Pennsylvania: Schiffer Publishing, 2002

Walk, John. *Big Book of Milk Glass*, Atglen, Pennsylvania: Schiffer Publishing, 2002.

Walk, John. *Fenton Glass Compendium 1940-1970*. Atglen, Pennsylvania: Schiffer Publishing, 2001.

Walk, John. *Fenton Glass Compendium 1970-1985*. Atglen, Pennsylvania: Schiffer Publishing, 2001.

Walk, John. *Fenton Glass Compendium 1985-Present*. Atglen, Pennsylvania: Schiffer Publishing, 2003.

Walk, John. *Fenton Rarities 1940-1985*. Atglen, Pennsylvania: Schiffer Publishing, 2002.

Walk, John. *Fenton Special Orders 1940-1980.* Atglen, Pennsylvania: Schiffer Publishing, 2003.

Walk, John. *Fenton Special Orders 1980-Present.* Atglen, Pennsylvania: Schiffer Publishing, 2003.

Whitmyer, Margaret and Ken. *Fenton Art Glass Company 1907 to 1939.* Paducah, Kentucky: Collector Books, 2003.

Whitmyer, Margaret and Ken. *Fenton Art Glass Company 1939 to 1980.* Paducah, Kentucky: Collector Books, 1999.

Catalogs

Fenton Art Glass Company. *Company Catalogs.* Williamstown, West Virginia: Fenton Art Glass Company, 1950-2004.

L. G. Wright Glass Company. *Company Catalogs.* New Martinsville, West Virginia: L. G. Wright Glass Company, 1960-70s.

Phil and Helen Rosso. *Company Catalogs*. Port Vue, Pennsylvania: Wholesale Glass Dealers, 1990s to 2004.

Periodicals

All About Glass: 2003- 2004
Butterfly Net: 1985- 2004.
Depression Glass Daze: 1970- 1997.
Fenton Flyer: 1995- 2004.
Fenton Nor'Wester: 1995- 2004.
Glass Collectors Digest: 1987- 1997.
Glass Messenger: 1996- 2004.
Glass Review: 1975- 1991.
Glory Hole: 1990- 2002.

Personal Correspondence

Ash, Shelley Fenton, Email to author, Fenton Art Glass Company, 2004

Burton, Frances. Email to author, Fenton Art Glass Company, 2004

Dick, Pam. Email & telephone conversation to author, Fenton Art Glass Company, 2004

Erb, Lynn Fenton, Email to author, Fenton Art Glass Company, 2004

Fenton, Christine. Email to author, Fenton Art Glass Company, 2004

Fenton, Frank M. Fenton. Letter & telephone conversation to authors, Fenton Art Glass Company, 2003

Fenton, George & Nancy. Letter and telephone conversation to authors, Fenton Art Glass Company, 2004

Fenton, Mike. Email to author, Fenton Art Glass Company, 2004

Fenton, Randy. Email to author, Fenton Art Glass Company, 2004

Fenton, Scott. Email to author, Fenton Art Glass Company, 2004

Fenton, Tom. Email to author, Fenton Art Glass Company, 2004

Hill, Amber, Bob and Pat. Email to author, Fenton Art Glass Company, 2004

King, Wayne. Email & telephone conversation to author, Fenton Art Glass Company, 2003

Maston, Jennifer. Email and telephone conversation to author, Fenton Art Glass Company, 2004

Saffell, Jon. Email & telephone conversation to author, Fenton Art Glass Company, 2004

Seufer, Howard. Email & telephone conversation to author, Fenton Art Glass Company, 2004

Walk, John. Email & telephone conversation to author, Fenton books author, 2004

Internet

Fenton Fanatics: www.fentonfan.com
John Gager, Webmaster

Index